CHAPTER ONE: HOMELESSNESS IN THE UK

Housing and homelessness

Homelessness – it's an emotive issue, and a lot of people have a lot to say about it. But what are the facts? And what is the Salvation Army doing about them in the UK? This page will give you an introduction to the subject.

In an ideal world everyone would have a place to live, somewhere to be part of a group or family, a structure for human life based on a place called home. The reality can be very different.

Society accepts that such basic resources as food, shelter, health care, education, security, love, support and understanding are essential to living a normal satisfying life. For many people these resources are provided within the home or family unit. Here young people can grow up satisfactorily with the added resource of links with other people and with access to other provisions in their wider community.

For a variety of reasons these support systems may break down at any time within a person's lifetime leaving someone to cope with often complex situations either in their own life or in that of someone else.

The issues are often dealt with individually for clarity, though life is usually far more complex and problems may be interrelated, e.g. homelessness may be caused by health problems or conversely homelessness is known to cause health problems.

In the United Kingdom there have been various attempts to define the reasons for and actual numbers of homeless people. For example, some people may become homeless because of broken relationships like divorce or not being accepted as part of a family; perhaps because of problems at home, possibly because of abuse, or because they have to live on a low income and find it hard to pay the rent.

There are those who define homeless people as 'runaways', 'throwaways' or 'growaways', the first definition covering that now smaller group of those who run away from the problems at home regardless of age or circumstances. However, most of the people on London streets, according to Centrepoint and others, are 'throwaways', people who have often spent much of their lives in institutions, have been thrown out of the last place where they lived and have no home to which they can return, should they wish to.

A major cause of homelessness is the shortage of good quality, suitable affordable housing in many areas. In 1995 it was reported in *Time to Move On* – a review of policies for single homeless people in London published by SHIL (Single Homeless In London) – that in London alone nearly 77,000 people were homeless or living in overcrowded accommodation, two-thirds of whom could have lived independently IF they had a home. The report revealed that just under 45,000 people were sleeping rough or had no permanent roof, and that a further 32,000 were living in overcrowded households

■ The above information is from the Salvation Army's web site: www.salvationarmy.org.uk

© *Salvation Army*

Introduction to homelessness

Information from CRASH

THE CONSTRUCTION AND PROPERTY INDUSTRY
CHARITY FOR THE HOMELESS

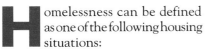

omelessness can be defined as one of the following housing situations:

- Without any accommodation e.g. sleeping rough.
- In temporary accommodation e.g. a shelter, hostel, B+B, squat.
- Staying temporarily with friends or relatives who are either unable or unwilling to provide accommodation in the longer term.

What causes homelessness?

There is no one single cause of homelessness, or any single description of a homeless person. However, there are several factors, which can lead to people being more vulnerable to losing their accommodation.

Lack of availability of affordable housing

Rent for both private and public housing have increased dramatically, making it hard for tenants on a low income to meet their rent requirements. House prices too have risen, and there has been a rise in the number of properties being repossessed.

Institutionalisation

Some people who leave institutions, such as the army or prison, or who have been in care as children, and move into their own accommodation struggle to look after themselves. This may be due to a lack of life skills, such as budgeting or cooking, emotional difficulties or loneliness and a lack of social support networks.

Mental health problems

Although mental health problems are not necessarily a direct cause of homelessness, they can contribute towards an individual having difficulties in maintaining a tenancy.

Substance misuse

Again, although drug and alcohol problems may not be the direct cause, they can certainly be implicated in the reasons why an individual becomes homeless. Substance misuse can also prevent them from successfully maintaining a new tenancy.

Life crises

Events such as bereavement, relationship breakdown and job loss can all lead to feelings of depression, isolation and loneliness. All of these can contribute to people being unable to cope and losing their accommodation.

The reasons why someone becomes homeless can be very complex, involving a combination of factors, which will be different for each individual.

Homelessness – the political agenda

The fall in the number of rough sleepers and the impact of the Homelessness Act 2002 has led many charities in the sector to reconsider the scope and purpose of their activities. The Act obliges Local Authorities to carry out a review of statutory and non-statutory homeless figures in their area. They must then submit a strategy to tackle the issues by 31st July 2003. The reduction in rough sleeping has led many organisations to re-focus on prevention work and several of the large national charities, such as Crisis and Shelter, are increasing their activity at local level. Meanwhile, locally based agencies are having to consider how to increase their capacity to work with their Local Authority, especially as the guidance issued with the Homelessness Act requires the Local Authority to include the voluntary groups working with homeless people in their consultations as they prepare their strategy. More about the Act can be found at the Shelter web site.

Homelessness acceptances by region

Region	Most recent figures		Comparison with previous year		
	Homeless households in priority need Jan-Mar 2003	Number per thousand, Jan-Mar 2003	Homeless households in priority need Jan-Mar 2002	Number per thousand, Jan-Mar 2002	% change on year
North East	1,920	1.8	1,470	1.4	+31%
North West	4,200	1.5	3,430	1.2	+22%
Yorks & Humber	3,950	1.9	2,870	1.4	+38%
East Midlands	2,080	1.2	1,940	1.1	+7%
West Midlands	3,930	1.8	3,950	1.8	-1%
East of England	2,910	1.3	2,640	1.2	+10%
London	8,120	2.6	7,220	2.3	+12%
South East	3,770	1.1	3,370	1.0	+12%
South West	3,300	1.6	2,840	1.4	+16%
Total	**34,170**	**1.6**	**29,730**	**1.4**	**+15%**

Source: ODPM, Crown copyright

Homelessness directorate

The Government has also set up a Homelessness Directorate, that brings together various initiatives. The Directorate incorporates the work of the Bed and Breakfast Unit, the introduction of the homelessness legislation, the production of the National Homelessness Strategy and the role of the Rough Sleepers Unit. Further information about this new directorate is available on the ODPM Housing web site.

Bed and Breakfast Unit

Following public consultation, the Bed and Breakfast Unit (BBU) has now set the target that no families with children should live in bed and breakfast hotels by March 2004, except in emergency.

Affordable Housing Unit

Increasing the supply of affordable housing is key to tackling homelessness in high demand areas. The Affordable Housing Unit has been established in the Government Office for London. It will work closely with the Homelessness Directorate.

Homelessness Act

After years of campaigning by the homelessness voluntary sector, a specific Homelessness Bill was enacted in February 2002. It broadened the categories of vulnerable people to whom Local Authorities have duty of care, but still left old people and pregnant women outside the net. CRASH will continue to highlight the needs of all homeless people and seek to ensure appropriate care is available.

Homelessness – Scotland

The Scottish Executive has a Homelessness Task Force chaired by the Social Justice Minister. This has

developed a radical approach to both prevention and alleviation of homelessness including eradication of priority needs and intentionality.

Intentionality: When someone leaves without a valid reason, for example is evicted as a troublesome neighbour who may also have an anti-social behaviour order placed on them stopping them returning to the area.

If they steadfastly refuse to accept offers of accommodation. Or the entrenched rough sleeper who tries to 'come in' gets a flat and then leaves because he is unable to be restricted within four walls.

Eviction for rent arears – frail, old single people can lose the plot: when the bureaucracy around their benefits becomes a problem they fall into arrears and then get an eviction notice.

Homelessness – Wales

The Welsh Assembly created a Homelessness Commission to advise on its policy and it has voted significant sums of money to Local Authorities to assist in developing appropriate strategies.

Research

Both the Scottish Homelessness Task Force and the Homelessness Commission in Wales have relied on the JRF/CRASH *Review of Single Homelessness Research* to inform their proceedings. Both bodies have commissioned research to plug some of the gaps identified in the Review. In England the Joseph Rowntree Foundation, in conjunction with CRASH and other homelessness agencies, sent a letter advocating similar work is put in hand by the ODPM's Research and Policy Unit. This has resulted in research being commissioned in black and minority ethnic (BME) homelessness, one of the gaps identified in the JRF/CRASH *Review of Single Homelessness Research* published in 2000.

There is no one single cause of homelessness, or any single description of a homeless person

---

CRASH is working with Homeless Link, the national 'umbrella' organisation, to create a Homelessness Research Observatory. This will become a repository and resource on homelessness research, seek to identify research gaps, co-ordinate research effort and develop best practices in the field.

■ The above information is from CRASH's web site which can be found at www.crash.org.uk

© CRASH 2003

Homeless families

Information from Barnardo's

Nowhere to go

Many families, single parents and young people have no home at all. Homelessness is a major problem in Britain today. Homelessness is the result of a range of circumstances, almost always related to poverty. The main cause of homelessness is the lack of safe accommodation that people can afford. Privately rented accommodation is often of poor quality, expensive and difficult to find. It is likely to be particularly unsuitable for families with children. In London, three-quarters of the homeless are families, and yet just half of the accommodation has two or more bedrooms.

Other reasons for homelessness include the breakdown of relationships, family and friends being no longer prepared to accommodate them, and debt.

Homeless people, especially if they beg on the streets, are often seen in a negative way by newspapers and television as well as by members of the public. People often say things like: 'He should get off his backside and find a job' or 'it's her choice', or even, 'they're all on drugs anyway, it's their own fault'.

Not everyone feels like that about homeless people. Many people realise that homelessness is not such a simple thing. Homeless people have many different kinds of problems such as broken or unhappy families, feeling lonely and afraid on the streets and the difficulties of staying healthy.

What other sorts of things have you heard people say about homeless people? What is your own view – is it their fault, are they making choices? Why might they be homeless in the first place? What sorts of things would be really difficult if you were homeless?

Homeless children

- Children are the largest single group of people affected by homelessness, but their needs are often overlooked.

Barnardo's
GIVING CHILDREN BACK THEIR FUTURE

- Being homeless can have a devastating effect on your education, health, safety and development.
- In 1999 more than 62,000 family groups were found temporary accommodation such as bed and breakfast by local authorities. Many thousands more have had to put themselves in bed and breakfast.
- Shelter – a charity working on behalf of homeless people – estimated that in 1998 there were more than 32,000 children living in temporary accommodation in England alone.

The effects of homelessness on children include:

Children are the largest single group of people affected by homelessness

---

- Lack of a safe place to play
- Unsettled school life
- Health and hygiene problems
- Emotional problems
- Loss of social and community support.

Homeless young people

- It is estimated that between 200,000 and 300,000 people under the age of 25 are homeless at some point each year.
- Young single people do not have a legal right to permanent housing.
- Large numbers of young people – those leaving care and those who have experienced family breakdown – have no choice but to try and cope on their own from the age of 16 or 17.
- Between a quarter and a third of young, homeless people have been in council care.
- Each year there's less and less private rented accommodation and social housing (council houses) so it's more and more difficult to find a place to live.

- The above information is from Barnardo's. See page 41 for their address details.

© Barnardo's

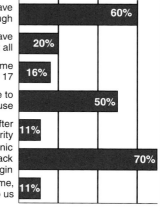

Youth homelessness

Every night Centrepoint provides a place to stay for over 500 homeless young people in its 14 London hostels, foyers and supported flats. Every young person who enters a Centrepoint hostel provides us with information relating to their background and their reasons for becoming homeless. Here we outline some key statistics compiled from this information.

Each year, almost 60% of the young people we see have slept rough — **60%**

Each year, over 20% of the young people we see have no qualifications at all — **20%**

16% of the young people we see have run away from home aged 16 or 17 — **16%**

Over 50% of the young people we see left home due to 'push factors' – conflicts, family breakdowns, evictions, abuse — **50%**

11% of the young people we assist have been looked after by a local authority — **11%**

70% of the young people we assist are black or of ethnic origin, however only 5% of the total UK population are black or of ethnic origin — **70%**

11% of the young people we see have no source of income, and cannot support themselves when they first come to us — **11%**

Source: Centrepoint

How many, how much?

Research summary into single homelessness and the question of numbers and cost. A Crisis and New Policy Institute research report

Background and focus of report

Homelessness in the United Kingdom has a broad legal definition that is pitched in terms of a person's entitlement to a home that is reasonable for them to continue to occupy. It is a definition that in theory could ensure that assistance and housing are offered to all homeless people. In practice, however, limitations on resources have necessitated the development of what is often described as a rationing system, whereby homeless people are judged on the basis of their perceived vulnerability.

Out of this has emerged the problem of single homelessness: strictly speaking, the homelessness suffered by single adults or couples without dependent children, although, in practice, overwhelmingly the former. The significance of single homelessness is that these people, unlike homeless adults with dependent children, are usually not owed what is known as the local authority's 'primary duty' towards homeless people, namely to provide them with accommodation.

The fact that they have been excluded by the legislation has meant that there has been a lack of priority in terms of both policy and research about their numbers and circumstances. It is this problem that is the

Fighting for hope for homeless people

focus of this study. More specifically, the study seeks to answer four questions:

- Is 'single homelessness' any longer a very helpful or even meaningful term?
- How many single homeless people are there?
- How much does single homelessness cost – and who bears that cost?
- What implications for policy arise from the findings on numbers and costs?

Key findings

1. Single homelessness remains a significant problem

Despite recent, welcome changes to the legislation, there is still a real need to recognise single homelessness. Recent guidance in England has increased the classes of person who can be deemed vulnerable and therefore in priority need. We expect that, as a result, more single homeless people will be classified as being in priority need than is the case now. However, we also expect that single homeless people will continue to make up the great bulk of those who are not deemed to be in priority need. Single homeless people therefore remain a group deserving of special attention and the term 'single homelessness' remains valid and powerful.

2. Single homelessness is in the hundreds of thousands at any one time

The research suggests a range of between 310,000 and 380,000. Only a tiny proportion of these – less than 1,000 – are rough sleepers. Around a quarter are single people staying either in hostels, bed and breakfast accommodation or facing imminent threat of eviction on the grounds of debt. The remaining three-quarters form what are known as concealed households, residing with friends or family but without any explicit right so to do and in accommodation that is, in some important way, unsatisfactory.

3. Individual homelessness costs thousands of pounds per year

The cost of an individual's homelessness can run to many thousands of pounds, suggesting that there may

be an economic case for spending money to reduce homelessness. Particular attention should be drawn to the scale and importance of recurring, time-related costs, such as the costs of temporary accommodation and the economic cost to society, as a whole, of unemployment associated with homelessness.

Numbers: single homelessness

The central technical challenge for this report has been to find a way of interpreting the definition of homelessness to allow it to be applied to the available sources of survey and administrative data. The following table outline the list of the groups Crisis concludes may be considered as single homeless, alongside our estimate of the number of people in Great Britain without dependent children in each group at any particular point in time.

Putting a cost on homelessness

The report represents the first attempt to quantify the costs that might be saved by reducing homelessness. This is calculated by providing estimates of the unit costs associated with particular episodes or incidents that arise in connection with homelessness. The costs that have been quantified in this report are those that usually fall upon institutions in the public, private and voluntary sectors. The cost categories that have been applied can be seen in the table [p. 6] which highlights costs associated with one particular case.

The report applied these unit costs to a number of scenarios, each of which (developed on the basis of the research literature and discussed with people working directly with homeless people) represents a particular possible pathway into, and sometimes through homelessness. In each individual case, the total cost of the scenario is sizeable – always thousands of pounds and sometimes tens of thousands. The report develops six case studies and applies six estimates of costs borne to each case. We have chosen Frank's story to highlight this methodology.

Despite recent, welcome changes to the legislation, there is still a real need to recognise single homelessness

Frank's story

Frank's story is one of six scenarios developed and costed in the report. It's a typical scenario covering 12 months from Frank's first experience of homelessness. The costs associated with this period are highlighted in the table [p. 7].

Frank had been married for 30 years and lived in London with his wife until she died unexpectedly. Frank found it difficult to cope, and with family living a long way from him, he felt very isolated. Frank was always a heavy drinker, but the new pressures made him drink even more. This compounded with redundancy made Frank very depressed.

Frank left the flat because the place was full of memories. He had also started receiving letters from his building society asking about mortgage repayments. Although Frank did not have much left to pay, he had no income, and could not handle the problem. He abandoned it and travelled to stay with his son in Sheffield for a week, but after that his son told him to leave. Frank also told his son he still had the flat, so his son didn't know that he had nowhere to go.

Frank did not want to go back to his flat, as he thought he might get arrested and did not know where else to go. So Frank ended up travelling to Manchester, where he slept rough. Other people living on the street told him about a day centre where he could go for food and advice and a night shelter which he started to visit.

Frank lived between the streets, night shelter and day centre for six weeks. His rough sleeping came to an end when a worker at the day centre noticed Frank was extremely ill. Frank had contracted TB, and was sent to hospital. The hospital also put him in touch with a social worker to help with his depression. They also put him in touch with a hostel.

In the hostel, Frank was given minimal level of support. Despite meeting with his key worker once a week, Frank's drinking problem and depression got worse – with nothing to do in the day, drinking was a means

The costs of Frank's homelessness

Cost category	Frank's case
Failed tenancy Includes: lost rent arrears; re-letting; possession order and eviction warrant; solicitor's fees; landlord's administration.	£3,000
Temporary accommodation Includes: hostel or refuge; bed and breakfast accommodation.	£10,500
Support services Includes: outreach worker; advice at hostel or day centre.	£2,000
Health services Includes: GP visit; services used after minor wounding; services used after serious wounding; treatment for mental ill health; treatment of TB; rehabilitation.	£7,000
Police and criminal justice Includes: in response to theft from a shop; in response to minor wounding; in response to serious wounding; prison.	£1,500
Potential resettlement Includes interview and processing; floating support	£500
Unemployment The value of the output lost (not produced).	nil
Total for 12 months	£24,500

of escape. As Frank was not entitled to local authority housing – as he was intentionally homeless – the hostel helped him into a shared flat, as there were no other options available. Frank moved in after six months at the hostel.

However, he only lasted three months in his new tenancy. His basic living skills were poor and he did not get on with the other people in the flat, who were always complaining about his drinking. A weekly visit from his key worker put him in touch with the local authority substance misuse team, but Frank did not use it. Embarrassed about returning to the hostel after leaving his flat, Frank went back to the streets.

Policy implications and recommendations

The scale of the problem and the costs associated with it demonstrate that policy makers and campaigning organisations need to treat the homelessness of adults without dependent children as a serious problem which should have a high priority. We conclude that the overall goal of policy should be to ensure that all homeless people should receive appropriate support to help them overcome their homelessness. This is deliberately wide and flexible to cover both the diverse needs that homeless people have themselves, and potentially the needs of those who help many of them by sharing their accommodation with them.

Providing appropriate support to all homeless people requires, we believe, a profound change both of policy and thinking. We have identified a range of challenges that must be addressed in order to bring about, or accelerate, the shift in policy that is needed. They are:

- In preparing to carry out their duties local authorities must ensure that they are gearing themselves up to operate on a scale that will allow them to tackle the full extent of the homelessness problem
- Government and local authorities should review service provision to ensure that it is able to address the problem of hidden homelessness

Single homelessness: the numbers

Single homelessness group	Numbers
Rough sleepers	800
Those who have been provided with supported housing (hostels/YMCAs/shelters)	around 25,000
Bed and breakfast and other boarded accommodation	around 50,000
People at imminent risk of eviction	around 2,000
Squatters	up to 10,000
Concealed households sharing overcrowded accommodation: (people who neither own nor rent the property they are living in and are neither the spouse, partner nor dependent child of the owner/renter)	
– Aged 25 and over or living with friends ('higher likelihood')	around 160,000
– Aged under 25 and living with family ('lower likelihood')	around 330,000
Concealed households sharing accommodation which is not overcrowded but where the head of household deems the arrangement unsatisfactory:	
– Aged 25 and over or living with friends ('higher likelihood')	around 60,000
– Aged under 25 and living with family ('lower likelihood')	around 120,000

These groups total some 750,000 but not all of them will be homeless. In order to produce an overall estimate of the number of single homeless people, it is necessary to make judgements about the proportion of each group likely to be homeless. On the basis of the characteristics of the different groups, we suggest a range for the overall number of single homeless people of between 310,000 and 380,000.

- Government, local authorities and the voluntary sector must improve their understanding of the true nature and extent of the problems facing single homeless people
- Government needs to consider what contribution improved employment opportunities could make to reducing the problem of single homelessness
- Government, local authorities and the voluntary sector should consider how best to recognise and support those families and friends who are providing accommodation to homeless people
- Government needs to examine whether the legislative framework and guidance that creates the distinction between single homeless people and families is compatible with ensuring that all homeless people receive the support that they need
- Government needs to ensure that

the resources are available to tackle the full extent of the homelessness problem

Get a copy of the full report

The full report is available free as a PDF download on the Crisis website: visit www.crisis.org.uk/downloads

Alternatively, contact the Crisis Policy team on 020 7426 3880 or email policy@crisis.org.uk.

Stay informed

Subscribe to the Crisis policy bulletin, the weekly round-up of hyperlinks to reports and statistics from around the homelessness and social exclusion sector. Visit www.crisis.org.uk/policybulletin to view and subscribe.

Crisis, 64 Commercial Street, London E1 6LT. Tel: 0870 011 3335. Fax: 0870 011 3336. Email: enquiries@crisis.org.uk Website: www.crisis.org.uk

© Crisis

Housing and homelessness

The facts in England. Information from Shelter. By Rita Diaz

Shelter is the largest national homelessness charity, with a network of over 50 housing aid centres and projects providing information, advice and advocacy for people in housing need. Shelterline is UK's 24-hour free national housing advice line.

Good housing is essential to the well-being of individuals but many people are affected by housing and homelessness problems. As a result their opportunities for employment, access to health care and education can also be affected.

Homelessness

Homelessness affects families and single people alike, and is the most acute indicator of a shortage of affordable housing.

Broadly, the homelessness legislation defines a person as homeless if 'there is nowhere where they (and anyone who is normally with them) can reasonably be expected to live'. We do not know the total number of people who are homeless according to this definition. Many people do not approach local authorities for help, because they do not know about their rights or because they think they won't get any help.

Of those who approach local authorities, 184,290 households were found to be homeless by local authorities in England in 2001. Shelter estimates that this represents over 440,000 people.

Of those found homeless, 118,700 households were in priority need and not intentionally homeless and local authorities have a duty to rehouse them. The remaining households are entitled only to advice and assistance. Nearly 70 per cent of households who are accepted for rehousing by local authorities are families with children or families that include a pregnant woman. Shelter estimates that about 100,000 children lived in households accepted as homeless during 2001. The rest are households

Shelter

without children who are considered to be 'vulnerable', because of age or mental or physical health problems.

People lose their homes for a wide range of reasons such as family relationship breakdown, domestic violence or eviction by a landlord.

Although people become homeless for many reasons, people who suffer discrimination and disadvantage are more likely to experience homelessness. For example in London during 2001, about a quarter acceptances were from African and Caribbean households, although they comprise only 11 per cent of households in London.

Single homelessness

The figures above are just the tip of the iceberg, there are no comprehensive national or local figures on the extent of homelessness among single people and couples without children. Most of these people have no priority for rehousing under the current homelessness legislation unless they can show they are 'vulnerable' (new regulations will extend the groups of people who qualify as vulnerable). Instead they are entitled only to advice and

assistance, the quality of which varies between authorities. During 2001, about 22,400 single homeless people contacted Shelter for help.

For some single homeless people, there will be no choice but to sleep on the streets. This is the most extreme and visible form of homelessness. The Government estimates that at the end of 2001 about 560 people were sleeping on the streets on any given night.

Temporary accommodation

Local authorities have a duty to provide temporary accommodation to homeless households who have a 'priority need'. Such accommodation can be within local authority's own stock, short-term housing from registered social landlords, or private landlords, hostels, or even in bed and breakfast accommodation.

At the end of March 2002 local authorities were housing 81,270 households in temporary accommodation. Of these, 11,820 were placed in bed and breakfast (B&B). This represents an increase of nine per cent from the same period in the previous year.

Homelessness Act 2002

This Act came into force in July 2002. It strengthens the homelessness safety net and places new

duties on local authorities to conduct a review of homelessness in their area and develop a strategy to tackle it. For more information log on to www.HomelessnessAct.org.uk

Provision of social housing

There is a shortage of good quality, affordable homes in this country. Increasingly, however, there are large variations in housing markets across the country with very serious shortages in some areas and surplus in others. Some regions, mainly London and the South East, have been hit harder by the lack of affordable housing. In order to meet both current and newly arising housing needs, Shelter estimates that around 90,000 affordable homes will be required each year. However, during 2000/01, only 18,000 units of social housing were completed.

Poor housing and empty homes

Poverty is a major barrier to obtaining good quality housing. The most economically and socially disadvantaged people in society tend to live in the worst housing. These groups include older people, lone parents, ethnic minorities and young people.

About 2.7 million households live in poor housing conditions. Of these, 750,000 are families with children. Nearly half a million households live in overcrowded conditions.

There are about 753,000 empty homes, 623,000 of which are in the private sector. This represents about four per cent of the total number of private sector properties.

Housing costs

The level of rent charged differs between the three rented sectors. Renting privately is the most expensive option. During 2000/01, the average weekly rent for:
- Private sector tenants was £84 and £133 in London
- Council tenants was £46 and £60 in London
- Registered social landlords' tenants was £56 and £66 in London.

The average house price is about £112, 400 and £214, 300 in London.

Paying for housing

Over the last two decades subsidy for housing has shifted from bricks and mortar investment to personal subsidies, mainly housing benefit. As a result housing expenditure has declined from £9,456 million in 1991/92 to £5,981 million in 2000/ 01. Over the same period the cost of housing benefit has increased from £7,419 million to £11,747 million.

About 3.2 million households receive housing benefit to help to pay their rent. The level of benefit people receive is often restricted. This can leave people without the means to pay their full rent. Restrictions in housing benefit affect mainly people renting privately. Research commissioned by the Government shows that 90 per cent of private tenants assessed for housing benefit reported shortfalls between their benefit entitlement and their rent. Of these, 70 per cent report shortfalls of £10 or more a week.

In 2000/01 the total gross expenditure on the provision of temporary accommodation for homeless households was about £356 million in England. Over £178 million of this total was spent on providing B&B accommodation. The cost of B&B provision has increased by 50 per cent over the last two years.

■ The above information is from Shelter's web site which can be found at www.shelter.org.uk Alternatively see page 41 for their address details.
© Shelter

Older people

Older people at risk of becoming the 'forgotten homeless'

Older people at risk of homelessness have become the 'forgotten homeless' according to a new report. The report, *Surviving at the margins: Older homeless people and the organisations that support them*, has found that older people's needs have been marginalised.

Over recent decades, homelessness initiatives have concentrated on more visible groups such as families and single young people. This, plus the fact that many older people are less vocal and demanding, has led to their marginalisation.

Joe Oldman, Help the Aged Homelessness and Housing Needs Manager, said: 'The needs of older homeless people are mostly ignored by mainstream service providers and not taken seriously by the Homelessness Directorate.'

Researcher Hazel Morbey, who co-authored the report, said: 'Older people who are homeless, or at risk of homelessness, have become the "forgotten homeless".

'The needs of these socially excluded people are absent or poorly represented in most policies aimed at older people, including housing and health strategies.'

A patchwork of complex circumstances and experiences can leave older people entrenched in very difficult situations and especially vulnerable. The research challenges popular myths of tramp-like figures, who choose a homeless life. While some end up living on the streets, many more live in poor or insecure housing situations where they risk becoming homeless.

However, voluntary organisations that work with older homeless people are chasing increasingly smaller amounts of time-limited money.

The report shows that funding is crucial for the voluntary services to maintain a good service and that training and links between voluntary, statutory and government organisations need to be improved.

It also recommends reforms to the benefits systems to address the problems identified by the research, some of which are already being introduced.

■ The above information is from Help the Aged's web site which can be found at www.helptheaged.org.uk
© Help the Aged 2003

Homelessness in Scotland

Information from Shelter – Scotland

What is homelessness?

Homelessness is being without a home. This seems an obvious thing to say but it needs to be said to emphasise that homelessness covers a wide range of situations. Think about what you mean when you talk about your home. It's somewhere warm and dry. It is also secure enough for you to store possessions, to welcome friends, to receive mail and to allow you to carry out many other aspects of daily life. It's about much more than a roof over your head.

There are only a few people in Scotland who sleep rough and are actually 'roofless'. No one is sure exactly how many people sleep rough each night. Shelter has previously estimated that, on any one night in Scotland, between 500 and 1,000 people will be sleeping on park benches, in graveyards, in derelict buildings, below bridges and so on and a Scottish Executive report in 1999 found that it could be as many as 11,000 in a year. However, a more recent piece of research commissioned by the Executive indicates that as few as 68 people could now be sleeping out each night. Shelter believes that the numbers do not matter: if even one person is forced to sleep rough this is too many. What is clear, however, is that many more people are living in situations where they do not have a home.

For example, in 2001-2, councils received over 46,000 homeless applications. Because some of these applications will have been the same families applying more than once, Shelter estimates that around 43,600 households applied for help as homeless last year. This represents an estimated 73,800 people. Most of these will not be sleeping rough but will instead be either effectively 'houseless' and having to live in places like temporary hostels and bed and breakfasts or sharing insecure and over-crowded conditions with other families. They may have been told by their bank or building society

Shelter
SCOTLAND

that they have to leave their own home because they cannot pay their mortgage. Or a landlord may have evicted them.

Even a number as large as 73,800 homeless people does not tell the full story. There are many other people who are described as 'hidden homeless'. This means that they are not visible in the way that someone sleeping on the streets is and it means that councils may not record them in official statistics. People in this situation include those sleeping temporarily on the floors or couches of friends and people living in out-of-season holiday lets or poor quality caravans in rural areas.

Who is homeless?

Sometimes people say that homeless people have particular problems, like mental ill health or issues with drug or alcohol misuse. People with these problems are very visible on our streets and need specialist help as well as a roof over their heads.

However, they make up a tiny percentage of the overall number of homeless. Some other homeless people need help for a short while if they are lucky enough to get a house;

for example, some young people. But most homeless people really need a home.

We know little about the backgrounds of people who sleep rough because they are a hard group for researchers to reach. But research by the Government suggests that almost all are single people. Only about one in five is a woman (it is much more dangerous for women to sleep rough – this may be because crime statistics show that women are more likely to be attacked). About a third of people sleeping rough are under the age of twenty-five. Few are from ethnic minorities.

Statistics collected by the Scottish Executive tell us a number of things about people who are homeless in the wider sense. In the six months between April and September 2002, about two-thirds of all those in households applying as homeless were adults. Of these, roughly half were men and half were women. 38% were adults between age 16 and 25 and 60% were between age 25 and 64. Of the 12,807 children who were part of households applying as homeless to Scottish councils in the first six months of 2002-3, 77% were under the age of 12. This is equivalent to 70 children a day or almost three children an hour.

It is, of course, much harder to tell who 'hidden homeless' people are. Shelter thinks that people from ethnic minorities, women and single people more generally are likely to be classified as hidden homeless. People who live in rural areas are also less likely to go formally to the council and declare themselves homeless so there may be more hidden homeless people in rural areas. However, in Scotland, unlike England there is very little tradition of homeless people taking over empty housing (or 'squatting'). This is partly because the law is different in Scotland to that in England and it has been easier to evict people who are occupying empty property.

Why do people become homeless?

The reasons why people become homeless are varied and illustrate that homelessness can happen to anyone. The figures also show that very seldom is it the individual or family that is the cause of their homelessness situation. Instead homelessness tends to occur because they can no longer continue to live somewhere or they have a dispute with a partner. The points below illustrate the main reasons given by people when they approach a local authority to apply as homeless. These are the immediate rather than the underlying causes. For example, the family may be homeless because they can't pay their rent, but the reason they give the local authority may be eviction.

The following were given as the main reason for applying as homeless by the 23,150 households that applied during the six months to September 2002:

- 24% dispute with a partner,
- 20% parents no longer able to accommodate them,
- 16% relatives or friends unable to accommodate them,
- 6% harassment or non-domestic violence,
- 6% had been discharged from prison,
- 5% loss of private tenancy,
- 4% lost accommodation in a hostel, lodgings or hotel.

These statistics show that homelessness is rarely the fault of the people who are homeless. Often they will have struggled to pay off debt for a long time before they are evicted or their home is repossessed. Other problems arise for people leaving institutions. For example, many young people who have been 'in care' because their parents cannot look after them become homeless. As they leave care they are often not prepared for how difficult living on their own will be and if problems arise they have no parents to turn to for help.

But the Scottish Executive's statistics don't tell the full story of why people become homeless. For example, the situation of one family sharing with another family and being asked to leave may just be the

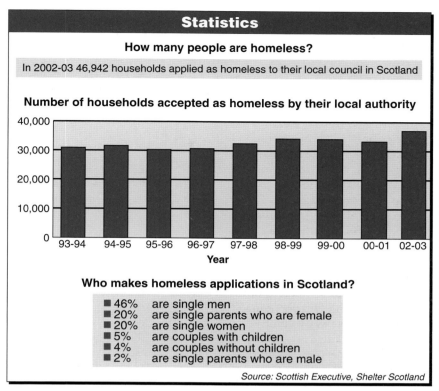

Statistics

How many people are homeless?

In 2002-03 46,942 households applied as homeless to their local council in Scotland

Number of households accepted as homeless by their local authority

Who makes homeless applications in Scotland?

- 46% are single men
- 20% are single parents who are female
- 20% are single women
- 5% are couples with children
- 4% are couples without children
- 2% are single parents who are male

Source: Scottish Executive, Shelter Scotland

last stage in a long episode of homelessness. The family may have earlier lost accommodation of their own and had to go to stay with friends as an emergency measure.

Even where families manage to obtain housing they may not be able to maintain it. Researchers working for the Scottish Executive have shown that around 27% of all applicants who apply to local authorities are making 'repeat applications'; in other words they have previously had to apply as homeless to a local authority. Between April and September 2002, around 5% of applications were from households who applied more than once during those six months. Just over 1% of the applicants applied more than three times during the period. This may be because they were allocated unsuitable housing or housing that did not meet their needs. We know that many repeat applicants have experienced relationship breakdown and/or domestic abuse and find it hard to find a permanent home to move on to after such experiences. In these and other cases housing allocations need to be sensitive to the needs of individuals and families and support may need to be provided.

The real problem is that there is not enough good housing around that

people can afford to pay for or enough support (such as advice on managing money, accessing benefits, accessing local facilities, and so on) available for people once they obtain a house or flat to ensure that they can manage it.

What can be done about homelessness?

Homelessness is a big problem in Scotland but it is not inevitable. In other words we should not accept that people have to sleep on the streets and in shared hostels because they have nowhere else to live. Homelessness can be solved if there is the right combination of housing and other types of help for homeless people. Shelter believes that at least 60,000 houses need to be built over the next five years. Some of these homes *could* be made available by renovation of empty property, but a lot of housing which is empty is in very poor condition or is far away from jobs so it may not be able to be brought back into use. If that is the case, the houses need to be newly built. But they must be affordable for people on low incomes and that means most of them being built for renting from councils or independent voluntary organisations called housing associations.

Increasing the number of affordable homes is the most important step that could be taken. Another important step is to ensure that everyone can afford to pay for their home no matter how low their income is. At the moment this is done through housing benefit. Over the last few years some people don't get housing benefit to cover all the money they pay in rent: for example, young single people who live in homes rented from a private landlord. People who own their own homes only get very limited help if they get into difficulties with their mortgage. Shelter thinks it makes sense to prevent homelessness by ensuring that everyone gets the same amount of help to pay his or her rent. Home-

> *We should not accept that people have to sleep on the streets and in shared hostels because they have nowhere else to live*

owners who get into difficulty should receive mortgage benefit.

There are a few other specific things that could be done to help tackle homelessness. Shelter thinks housing education should be like careers education in schools so that young people are prepared for the realities of leaving home whenever

they eventually do this. Independent information and advice centres should be opened in every part of Scotland so that people can have a chance to talk about housing problems before they lead to homelessness. Some people who need special help with housing should have a plan drawn up when they first get a home of their own. The plan would set out the types of help they need, whether it is advice about how to look after a house, about paying the rent and other bills or it could be about care or health needs that they have.

■ The above information is from Shelter Scotland. See page 41 for their address details.

© Shelter Scotland

Causes and effects of homelessness

Information from Off the Streets and into Work (OSW)

The causes and effects of homelessness are widely discussed. Often these are interchangeable, for example unemployment could have caused someone to lose their home, but unemployment could also be the result of becoming homeless.

Figures from the Office of the Deputy Prime Minister (ODPM), detailing priority homeless acceptances for the second quarter of 2003, reveal that triggers for homelessness broke down as follows:

■ 35% because parents, relatives or friends were no longer able or willing to accommodate them
■ 19% were due to a breakdown of a relationship with a partner
■ 14% were due to an end of an assured short-hold tenancy
■ 5% due to the loss of other rented or tied housing
■ 2% due to mortgage arrears
■ 2% due to rent arrears
■ 23% due to other reasons

In more general terms, the homeless population tend to have a higher incidence of the following than the population as a whole:
■ Physical and/or mental health problems

Off the Streets and into Work

■ Substance misuse
■ Unemployment
■ Basic skills needs
■ Dyslexia and other learning difficulties
■ Experience of sexual or physical abuse
■ Have spent time in care
■ Have spent time in the armed forces
■ Experience of the criminal justice system
■ Relationship breakdown
■ Problems accessing welfare benefits

Homeless people are a very disadvantaged and excluded group and this is highlighted in a number of ways:
■ Difficulties in accessing social housing or private rented housing
■ High rents in hostels can cause difficulties in finding work

■ Temporary accommodation (such as hostels) are often difficult and insecure environments to live in, to establish routines or to plan ahead
■ Poor access to medical services
■ Difficulties in opening bank accounts and access to other mainstream services
■ Stigma and harassment
■ Discrimination
■ Poverty

Without support, this can affect homeless people in a number of ways:
■ Loss of self-esteem
■ Becoming institutionalised
■ Deterioration of mental and physical health
■ Increase in substance misuse
■ Loss of ability and will to care for oneself
■ Increased danger of abuse and violence
■ Increased chance of entering the criminal justice system
■ Development of behavioural problems

■ The above information is from Off the Streets and into Work's (OSW) web site: www.osw.org.uk

© Off the Streets and into Work (OSW)

Lost from view

A study of missing persons in the UK

By Nina Biehal, Fiona
Mitchell and Jim Wade

Thousands of people are reported missing each year, yet very little is known about who they are, why they disappear and what happens to them. Researchers at the University of York have completed the most extensive study of going missing in the UK. Drawing on case records on nearly 2,000 adults and young people reported to the National Missing Persons' Helpline and questionnaires completed by 114 formerly missing people, this is the first study to unravel the meaning of going missing across the entire spectrum of missing persons' cases.

'I just thought the family would be better off without me around, so I just slipped out of the picture without telling anyone.'

People of any age may go missing, from very young children to people in their 90s. Among adults, men are reported missing far more frequently than women, whereas young runaways are more likely to be female. Those most likely to be reported missing are:

- girls aged 13-17
- men aged 24-30.

After age 30, the proportion reported missing declines progressively as age increases.

Most people go missing intentionally, to escape family or other problems, but others may not make a deliberate decision to leave.

Age has a bearing on the likelihood of going missing deliberately. Although people may deliberately go missing at any age from middle childhood, teenagers and adults under the age of 60 are more likely to go missing intentionally than people of other ages.

Why adults go missing
Decided 64%
Relationship breakdown
Escape problems
Escape violence
Mental health problems

Drifted 19%
Lost contact
Transient lifestyle

Unintentional 16%
Dementia
Mental health problems
Accident/ harm
Miscommunication

Forced 1%
Victim of crime

Most adults decided to leave due to a breakdown in their relationships with partners or parents. In con-sequence, they were missing to other important people in their lives too, often for many years. In particular, fathers lost contact with their children when they disappeared after marriage breakdown. Similarly, women fleeing domestic violence broke off contact with children, parents or siblings due to fear of being traced. Some left to escape an accumulation of personal, financial, or mental health problems, while others disappeared following a breakdown in their mental health or in order to commit suicide.

Most of those who drifted out of touch had lost contact as a result of moving away. However, this apparent drift out of contact some-times appeared to be a form of avoidance, to escape unacknow-ledged family problems. Others drifted out of contact due to their transient lifestyles, occasioned by mental health, drug or alcohol problems. Living at the margins of society, this socially excluded group moved between sleeping rough and periods in hostels or other temporary accommodation.

The majority of adults who went missing unintentionally were people aged 60 and over suffering from dementia. Most other unintentional absences were linked to depression or to psychotic illnesses, where medication had been missed.

Why children and young people go missing

Over two-thirds of young people under 18 left deliberately. The majority were teenagers running away from home, in most cases due to conflict with parents but some-times in order to escape abuse, or due to problems at school. Some 16- to 17-year-olds left due to a breakdown in relationships with parents, often remaining missing for several years.

'The reason I ran away was because I was sick and tired of ending up black and blue from the beatings dad used to give me and my sister.'

One in ten children were missing unintentionally, usually because they had become separated from a parent or siblings as a consequence of family breakdown. One in twelve, however, had been forced into going missing, either due to parental abduction or because they had been thrown out by a parent and had subsequently disappeared.

Who is at risk of going missing?

Adults are more likely to go missing if they are going through a crisis or a difficult transition or they are vulnerable due to chronic difficulties. People in crisis may go missing in an attempt to resolve or escape from difficulties arising from family problems, bereavement, health/mental health or financial problems.

For some young adults, the transition to adult status leads to conflicts over autonomy or the choice of a partner which, if not resolved, may prompt them to go missing. The transition from institutions such as children's homes, prisons or the armed forces may also result in going missing, as those who are not adequately supported may drift into a transient lifestyle. People who are vulnerable due to dementia or other mental health problems, learning disabilities or drug or alcohol dependency are also at risk of going missing.

The dangers of going missing

Missing people are at risk of sleeping rough. Around two-fifths of young runaways and 28% of the adults surveyed had slept rough while missing and almost one-third of young runaways had stayed with a stranger. Some experienced other dangers, including physical or sexual assault. Many also reported experiencing emotional distress and isolation.

There is also a real danger that going missing can lead to an unintended long-term severing of family relationships. Some reported that it was hard to approach their families again due to feelings of shame or fear of rejection.

Time missing

The likelihood of being traced decreased as time progressed. Among those traced, time missing was linked to reasons for leaving. Young runaways and adults missing unintentionally were usually found within six months and often much sooner. Children separated from relatives due to family breakdown and adults who left due to relationship breakdown, or who drifted out of contact, could be missing for years.

Outcomes of going missing

Among those who were found alive, only 20% returned. Most of these were young runaways and people who had gone missing unintentionally due to dementia or mental health problems. However, return was unlikely to be an option for many, especially where they had been missing for many years. Around two-fifths of those traced were happy to renew contact with relatives, but a similar proportion did not, indicating the seriousness of the rift with their families.

Among those who were found dead, one-half had committed suicide and one-third had died as a result of coming to harm or an accident. The majority of suicides were male, as were most of the vulnerable people who came to harm while missing.

Issues for policy and practice

Promoting greater public awareness of what it means to be missing may help to secure a more favourable climate for the support of missing people, their families and friends.

The availability of information about local and national services is a concern. Publicity about services should also address the full spectrum of missing cases.

A better understanding of groups that may be at particular risk and of the range of circumstances that make going missing more likely, should help alert practitioners to needs and sharpen preventive

---

Around two-fifths of young runaways and 28% of the adults surveyed had slept rough while missing

---

responses. Advice and information, counselling and mediation made available at an early point may help individuals seek alternative strategies for managing their problems.

Young runaways and many adults who leave suddenly need direct access to safe supported accommodation to avoid exposure to the streets. Those not intending to return may need other forms of help to rebuild their lives.

Families of missing people have continuing needs for advice, practical help and emotional support, including access to professional counselling in some cases.

Where families lose touch, agencies that undertake social tracing tend to be highly valued by them. Services that facilitate direct or indirect communication between missing people and their families can be successful in mediating return or reconciliation. At the very least, a simple 'safe and well' message can alleviate the worst fears of families.

Missing persons' schemes are being developed to provide follow-up support to young runaways once they have returned. It may also be the case that many adults and their families could benefit from an opportunity to explore underlying issues that may have prompted an absence, including opportunities for counselling and mediation.

There are no reliable estimates of the scale of the missing problem. A single comprehensive database is needed to record all missing cases, including both vulnerable and non-vulnerable cases.

The missing issue requires a co-ordinated lead from central government to provide a clear policy direction and to ensure that the needs of missing people are reflected in all departmental initiatives. A national forum, linking statutory and voluntary agencies with an interest in this area, could lead to the development of more integrated policy and service responses.

■Research undertaken in partnership with the National Missing Persons' Helpline and funded by the Nuffield Foundation.

Homeless people's health

Information from St Mungo's

Homeless people are much more likely to be mentally and physically ill than the rest of the population. Many went on the street because they were mentally ill, or were heavy drinkers or drug addicts; others will have developed these problems while sleeping rough. This page looks at their problems, and our response.

Physical health problems

- People sleeping rough have a rate of physical health problems that is two or three times greater than in the general population.
- These problems include: chronic chest and breathing problems, wounds and skin complaints, musculo-skeletal problems and digestive problems.
- The rate of tuberculosis among rough sleepers and hostel residents is 200 times that of the known rate among the general population.
- Rough sleepers aged between 45 and 64 have a death rate 25 times that of the general population.

(St Mungo's helps those with physical health problems by ensuring they see a GP, and by employing resident nurses and visiting doctors).

Mental health problems

- The Government's Social Exclusion Unit estimates that 30 to 50 per cent of people sleeping rough suffer from mental health problems, which, for about 88 per cent, existed before they went on the street.

(St Mungo's helps people with mental health disorders by ensuring they can see a GP and psychiatrist. We also employ a specialist mental health team which assesses residents and ensures appropriate treatment. We use the services of counsellors where appropriate.)

Drug and alcohol problems

- About half of people sleeping rough are heavy drinkers and about one in seven are drug addicts.

(St Mungo's helps people with drink and drug problems by ensuring they can see a GP. We also employ a specialist alcohol and drug team which assesses residents and ensures appropriate treatment. We run a specialist detoxification unit and a special unit for drug users.)

Notes

- 'People sleeping rough have a rate of physical health problems that is two or three times greater than in the general population' – from *Homes for Street Homeless People*, DETR, 1999.
- 'The rate of tuberculosis among rough sleepers and hostel residents is 200 times that of the known rate among the general population' – from *Rough Sleeping*, Social Exclusion Unit, Cabinet Office, 1998.
- 'Rough sleepers aged between 45 and 64 have a death rate 25 times that of the general population' – from *Rough Sleeping*, Social Exclusion Unit, Cabinet Office, 1998.
- 'The Government's Social Exclusion Unit estimates that 30 to 50 per cent of people sleeping rough suffer from mental health problems' – from *Rough Sleeping*, Social Exclusion Unit, Cabinet Office, 1998.
- 'About half of people sleeping rough are heavy drinkers and about one in seven are drug addicts' – from *Beyond Help*, J. O'Leary, 1997, National Housing Alliance.

■ The above information is from St Mungo's web site which can be found at www.mungos.org

© St Mungo's

Rough sleepers

The table below lists by local authority the 30 areas in the country with the highest current concentrations of rough sleepers per night

Local authority	No.	Local authority	No.
Westminster	234	Chester	26
Camden	66	Croydon	25
Oxford	52	Waltham Forest	20
Lambeth	46	Slough	20
Manchester	44	Gloucester	20
Birmingham	43	Brent	19
Brighton and Hove	43	Exeter	19
City of London	36	Bournemouth	18
Bristol	32	York	18
Nottingham City	31	Ealing	18
Stoke-on-Trent	31	Leeds	17
Cambridge	31	Penrith	17
Liverpool	30	Richmond upon Thames	16
Kensington and Chelsea	28	Hammersmith and Fulham	16
Southwark	26	Watford	15
		Total	**1,057**

Source: The Salvation Army

Mean streets

**A fifth of Britain's 400,000 homeless have mental health problems.
Mark Gould reveals the difficulties faced by their outreach workers**

For an army of homeless mentally ill men and women, the parks, cemeteries and open spaces of London are the places where they live, sometimes for decades, hidden yet in plain view of 'normal society'. There are also 400,000 hidden homeless people in the UK living in squats, hostels, B&Bs and 'on friends' floors', according to the homeless charity Crisis. Around one-fifth have severe mental health problems, such as schizophrenia, manic depression and addiction to drugs or alcohol.

Many of these people are reclusive and refuse help. In an attempt to tackle the problem, the NHS and the government's Rough Sleepers Unit have funded a network of outreach teams of nurses, social workers and doctors. They have the sometimes heartbreaking and physically dangerous job of trying to provide psychiatric care and accommodation for people who have rejected society.

The Focus team, part of Camden and Islington mental health and social care trust, has one of the toughest and busiest patches in the UK, stretching from King's Cross to Hampstead Heath. On their weekly outreach sessions to find and diagnose new patients and check on old friends, the team distribute food, drinks, cigarettes and, in winter, sleeping bags and blankets.

It's already hot and sticky at 7am as community psychiatric nurses Emma Bates and Rachel Humber make their first call of the day to a small igloo made of plastic sheets in a building-site car park. Raphael has lived here for three years. He has a wife and kids somewhere, but he is convinced that bureaucrats are lying to him. That is tricky because Rachel wants to get him rehoused and that means meeting local housing officers.

He greets us with a handshake and a smile, but he soon gets on to his main obsession. 'I have written to all the main political parties about

my case and the prime minister is aware of it. I want an investigation into how they have lied in two letters.' Eventually, after 20 minutes of persuasion, he agrees to meet the council. A small victory.

Although mentally ill, Raphael has never been ill enough to be 'sectioned' – forcibly detained under the Mental Health Act – and he has refused to be seen by a psychiatrist. Rachel says that it is common for people to refuse even basic help. 'One man would only wear a thin shirt and raincoat in the winter and say it was God's will that he lived. People are fantastically resilient.' The team have 120 people on their books at any one time, with varying levels of mental illness.

Last year they admitted 27 people to hospital – 15 for urgent treatment. They also managed to find housing for 90 people – either moving them from the street or from squats – and 37 of these went on to do courses or vocational training. But 20 men and women simply went missing, 15 refused to leave the streets and five who had been rehoused returned to the street.

The charity Shelter says that the average life expectancy of a homeless person is 42. But the park rangers on Hampstead Heath estimate that Harry, a recluse in his

sixties, has lived there in a derelict concrete windbreak, for at least 30 years. Social worker Louise Cantrell says that while Harry is mentally ill he gets by on food from soup kitchens and handouts from sandwich shops. 'He does not represent a danger to himself or anyone else. He is very private and nervous of others, but he is an individual and has rights.' Louise is an approved social worker with the power to section patients. She is acutely aware of the importance of distinguishing between those who are ill and those who are odd and eccentric. 'You don't want to normalise them for the sake of it just because they don't fit in with "normal" society.'

Michael, who is about 50, but looks 70, is not certain how long he has lived on Hampstead Heath. 'I have been here five, six, seven or eight years,' he says before launching into a ramble about boarding a ship in Wales.

Part of the Focus team's work involves days and sometimes months just saying hello and checking and assessing. Michael has a family somewhere, but he has been an alcoholic for decades and has brain damage as a result. His pot belly gives the impression that he is well fed, but the team have a gloomier prognosis and think it's his liver.

The route to Steve's home is easy to spot because he has stencilled his name on the pavements and walls nearby. Steve, who is schizophrenic, has spent several years living in derelict cars and vans. His latest home is a van on flat tyres. Emma Bates taps gently on the window. There is movement within and eventually Steve opens the rusty door to reveal a jumble of clothes, plastic toys and sheets. Painfully slowly he climbs out. 'This is private property you know. You are trespassing.'

Steve stares at the floor and refuses to answer questions. Suddenly he gathers up two massive bags and just walks off. Emma is only too aware that the very act of approaching people like Steve feeds their paranoia. 'It's a tragedy, but what else can we do? We have to find out how people are, but sometimes that can be just as traumatic for them.'

> **'It's a tragedy, but what else can we do? We have to find out how people are, but sometimes that can be just as traumatic for them'**

We catch sight of Steve several times on our rounds, a big unkempt man standing and staring into the middle distance as the world hurries by. A week later he was sectioned for his own safety but later managed to escape. The Focus team are still looking for him.

The heartbreaking nature of the Focus team's work becomes clear in a lovely terracotta street where Jane is tending to her window boxes. For three years she has lived on the steps outside the house that was home for 40 years. After her husband's death she was evicted. The property was sold to a developer who boarded up and padlocked the doors and windows. The neighbours say she is the victim of a gross injustice and it's difficult to disagree.

Local newspaper coverage has made her a cause célebre. Surrounded by her flowers and possessions, in a jumble of plastic bags and packing cases, she has slept outside winter and summer, sun and rain, except for a brief spell in hospital. She is a fiercely independent woman with a glint in her eye and a strong handshake. She knows everyone in the street, runs errands for them and walks their dogs. Jane refuses offers of everything from a cup of tea to a roof over her head with a determined monologue.

'Go and give these things to people who need them, people who have fought in two world wars. I don't need anything from you. I wouldn't take anything from the people that put me in a madhouse. All I want is to get back in that house. I am nothing now. If you kill me I would not bleed.'

But the team are happy. They can see that Jane is clean, well fed and relatively stable. However, Emma and Louise know that the day will come when she faces the trauma of eviction from her former doorstep. 'The property developer will lose patience. We have to be around when that happens. That is what this is all about.'

■ Some of the names in this article have been changed to protect identities

■ This article first appeared in *The Observer*, 7 September, 2003.

© Mark Gould

Research challenges homelessness stereotypes

A new three-year study by Safe in the City to understand how young people and their carers view homelessness will begin in September 2003. This study, in collaboration with London Metropolitan University, has been made possible through a £155,659 grant received by the Community Fund.

Research findings are expected to influence how services to prevent homelessness target those who are hardest to reach as well as dealing with social exclusion issues.

Safe in the City is leading the prevention of youth homelessness through an action research programme that provides support and looks at what works best.

The charity co-ordinates seven 'cluster schemes' that work with young people at risk of homelessness and their parents. Each cluster scheme provides intensive packages of support joining family work, skills and education programmes and personal development work into one service. Safe in the City monitors their progress to ensure the services are effective.

Marcia Brophy, research manager, Safe in the City, said: 'This study is different because we will talk to a variety of young people and their parents/carers who are "at risk" rather than already homeless. It will give us a comprehensive understanding of their perceptions, experiences and stereotypes of homelessness. We can use this information to develop future homelessness prevention services, making them more accessible to those in most need.'

The Community Fund's Research Grants Programme awarded a total of £855,000 to help thousands of young people by looking at issues including: family change; homelessness; poverty; student suicide; and social problems.

Diana Brittan, Chair of the Community Fund, said: 'The grants awarded to Family Mediation Scotland, Safe in the City, the Buttle Trust, Papyrus and the Howard League will ultimately improve thousands of young people's lives. Each research project will, I hope, enable a better understanding of young people's needs and will help to design better services to help them through difficult times.'

■ The above information is from Safe in the City's web site which can be found at www.safeinthecity.org.uk

© Safe in the City

The needs of homeless people

Information from St Mungo's

Family background

The reasons people begin sleeping rough are varied: each homeless person has his own story, or in some cases, her own story. Nevertheless, we know that many have had difficult family backgrounds:

- between a quarter and a third of people on the street have been looked after by local authorities while they were children
- of those in hostels for the homeless, 40 per cent have one or more indicators of disordered family background: being in care, being sent to a young offenders' institute, being suspended or expelled from school or being fostered or adopted.

We believe that many homeless people's difficulties in later life begin here. Poor parenting, parents who themselves are heavy drinkers or neglectful or abusive, can set bad examples for their children's behaviour. Some rough sleepers go on the streets after leaving home following a dispute with parents.

Becoming homeless

This type of family background can lead to difficulties relating to other people, heavy drinking, drug abuse and mental illness. These problems, coupled with difficulties finding suitable housing and unemployment, lead to homelessness. When rough sleepers were asked what the trigger was for them first becoming homeless, the most common reasons given were:

- relationship breakdown = 39%
- heavy drinking = 21%
- losing job = 18%
- having no money to pay for housing = 13%

Staying homeless

Those rough sleepers who do not have a drink, drug or mental health problem may find that the conditions on the streets create one. It is estimated that:

> *The reasons people begin sleeping rough are varied: each homeless person has his own story*

- over half have mental health problems
- around a half have drink problems
- and a fifth have a drugs problem

Notes

- 'Between a quarter and a third of people on the street have been looked after by local authorities while they were children' – from *Homes for Street Homeless People*, DETR, 1999, page 20.
- 'Of those in hostels for the homeless, 40 per cent have one or more indicators of disordered family background' – from St Mungo's internal survey of 146 of its residents in May 1997.
- The facts featured in the Becoming Homeless section are from an NOP survey commissioned by St Mungo's of 137 people sleeping rough in November 1998.
- The facts featured in the Staying Homeless section are from *Homes for Street Homeless People*, DETR, 1999, page 20.

■ The above information is from St Mungo's web site which can be found at www.mungos.org Alternatively, see page 41 for their address details.

© St Mungo's

Homelessness statistics

Information from Off the Streets and into Work (OSW)

Off the Streets and into Work

A lack of consensus on the definition of homelessness has compounded difficulties in estimating true figures on the number of people who are homeless, and the characteristics of homeless people.

Statutory homelessness

Government statistics tend to reflect only those who are accepted by local authorities under the specific criteria of homeless legislation as having priority need. In general this has usually meant unintentionally homeless households with dependent children, as well as some other specified vulnerable groups. Recent changes in guidance from the government have widened the groups of people who can be deemed vulnerable, however, and there has been a consequent rise in the number of people counted as homeless.

The total number of acceptances of homeless households in priority need for 2001/2 was 118,360, or 5.6 per 1,000 households. In London the total number was 31,130, or 9.8 per 1,000 households. There has been a year-on-year increase since 1997/98.

The primary reasons for acceptances of priority needs, according to second quarter 2003 Office of the Deputy Prime Minister (OPDM) figures, were:

- 52% due to a dependent child
- 10% as a household member became pregnant
- 9% due to mental illness
- 8% for young persons (16/17-year-olds and 18-20-year-old care leavers)
- 5% due to physical disability
- 4% due to domestic violence
- 3% due to old age
- 1% were homeless in an emergency
- 8% for other reasons

Single homelessness

Single homeless people are defined as those suffering from homelessness who are single adults or couples without dependent children. Because they do not have dependent children, single homeless people are far less likely to be deemed as having a priority need in terms of local authority housing provision. Therefore, they are unlikely to be represented in the above figures.

Nevertheless, it is estimated that the actual number of single homeless people at any one point is between a range of 310,000 and 380,000. Of these . . .

- Only a tiny proportion are rough sleepers – about 800
- About a quarter are single people staying in hostels, bed and breakfast accommodation or face imminent threat of eviction on the grounds of debt
- Three quarters form what are known as concealed households, residing with friends or family but without explicit right to do so and in accommodation which is,

in some important way, unsatisfactory

There is a much higher incident of single homelessness in London compared with the national average. Source: *How many, how much? Single homelessness and the question of numbers and cost.* A report for Crisis by Peter Kenway and Guy Palmer from the New Policy Institute.

Other single homeless research has revealed that:

- in most settings men heavily outnumbered women by around 4 to 1
- about half of men were aged between 30-49 years and at least half of women were aged under 30 years
- mental health and substance misuse problems are prevalent amongst all age groups

Source: *Single Homeless People in London. Profile of Service Users and Perceptions of Needs.* Maureen Crane and Anthony M. Warnes. Sheffield Institute for Studies of Ageing. University of Sheffield. Commissioned by Bondway Housing Association, St Mungo's and Thamesreach.

Ethnicity

All of the research carried out by various organisations shows that there is a higher incidence of homelessness amongst non-white ethnic groups. For example, the second quarter 2003 ODPM figures show that 71% of priority acceptances were classified as white, 9% were from African/Caribbean households, 5% from Indian/Pakistani/Bangladeshi households, 8% from other ethnic origin households and the remaining 6% from households where ethnic origin was not known. Source: ODPM website

■ The above information is from Off the Streets and into Work's (OSW) web site which can be found at www.osw.org.uk
© Off the Streets and into Work (OSW)

Home truths

Information from Streetlevel

What do homeless people look like?

Just take some time to think about that . . . Do any of the following thoughts spring to mind?

- shabby clothes
- sleeping in cardboard boxes
- drunkenness
- begging for money
- smelly
- won't hold down a job
- old
- addicted to drugs

Sometimes these things do describe homeless people, but they are all stereotypes and that means that they are not true of all homeless people and sometimes not true at all.

Let me explain what I mean by the word stereotype. Stereotypes are the way we define things just by looking at them using first judgements without getting to know the way that things really are.

For example, I have been homeless, and you might have seen me on the streets. But if you saw me, you might have thought that I took drugs, got drunk or begged – but I never did.

I sometimes slept in a cardboard box because it was cold, and my clothes got shabby because I was sleeping on the ground. But people looked at me like I didn't belong on the same street as them but if they had stopped to get to know me, they would have found out a different story to the one they were expecting.

The truth is that we are all unique, we all have different life stories and you simply can't group people together without making assumptions.

Imagine a smart young girl on the train next to you. She might be going to work or college now, but she might have been homeless one year ago, in fact she might still be living in a squat or a hostel. Or you might see someone on the street and think they got there because they were lazy, addicted to drugs or something, when really there is a very different story to their lives – maybe their parents moved to another country or threw them out onto the streets.

So next time you think about homeless people, or see someone asleep in a doorway, think about how they might have ended up there without relying on stereotypes or preconceptions.

Think about how you would want people to treat you, or look at you, or talk to you if you ever become homeless. It could have been you instead of them – or it could happen to you or someone you know!

Not all homeless people sleep on the streets

This is the most important home truth about homelessness that almost no one realises. Did you know that you are classed as homeless by the government if you are living in insecure housing such as a bedsit, a squat or a hostel, or even if you are moving round the houses of your friends or family?

You don't have to be sleeping on the streets to be classed as homeless. Street homelessness (sleeping rough) is only the visible part of being homeless and for many it is the worst.

Who is responsible?

A lot of people believe that when a person becomes homeless that it's

Perspectives on people who beg

All those who were interviewed were read out a list of statements relating to begging and were asked to indicate the extent to which they agreed or disagreed with them. The table below summarises all the statements comparing the opinions of the people who give money to beggars in comparison to those who do not.

	Total sample (208)		Never given money (144)		Has given money to beggars (64)	
	Agree	Disagree	Agree	Disagree	Agree	Disagree
I would not give money if I thought it would all be spent on drink or drugs	91%	8%	96%	4%	81%	16%
I would rather give money to a charity	82%	12%	93%	5%	60%	28%
I resent being approached by those begging	79%	17%	85%	12%	66%	30%
Those begging should try harder to find jobs	70%	16%	76%	11%	56%	25%
Most who beg have no other form of income	34%	58%	25%	68%	54%	36%
Most people who beg do not want to change their lives	53%	32%	53%	21%	31%	54%
People only beg as a last resort	46%	51%	35%	62%	70%	26%
Most people who beg are homeless	45%	48%	34%	59%	67%	23%
Those who beg are lazy	47%	42%	56%	34%	28%	62%

Source: DTLR, Crown copyright

Young runaways

Why do children and young people run away, or become homeless?

For most young people, running away is not something they have planned.

Deciding to run is a decision made on the spur of the moment, and the young person is often not prepared, with no money, no warm clothes, no phone numbers, nor any idea about where they might seek help.

Some of the main reasons children and young people run away, or find themselves homeless are:

Arguments

Jeannie, who was 16, asked ChildLine to call the police because her mum and dad had told her to leave. At ChildLine's request, the police collected her and returned her to her parents, who hugged her and agreed to talk the problem over.

Many of the children and young people who call ChildLine about running away or being homeless have argued with their families. Most desperately want to re-establish good communication and get on again with their parents and siblings.

Violence within the family

Kelly, 14, had run away after an argument with her mum, who had accused her of taking money from her purse, hit her and told her to pack her bags. Kelly had walked around all night and went back in the morning to talk to her mum, who hit her again, and pushed her to the ground. Kelly asked if she could go into care.

Some young people at risk of running away or becoming homeless are experiencing violence. When talking about their families, they describe being shouted at, sworn at, blamed for everything, scapegoated, hit, pushed, shoved and threatened by their parents or step-parents.

Pregnancy

'I'm pregnant and I don't want my mum to find out. I've run away to another town. I just can't face my mum.'

ChildLine
0800 1111

Young women who are pregnant can also face being thrown out by angry and aggressive parents. Sometimes they decide to run away rather than talk to their parents. Girls as young as 13 or 14 called ChildLine saying they had been thrown out of their homes after telling their parents they were pregnant.

Physical and sexual abuse

Jenny, 14, had run away with her friend Moira. Her dad had started to sexually abuse her when she was 10 and she couldn't stand it any more. She said: 'Mum didn't believe me so I told my auntie. She did believe me,

Around 37% of boys and 63% of girls calling about running away or being homeless also talked of being abused, physically and/or sexually

but she couldn't do anything about it. I'm scared he 'll come looking for me.'

Around 37% of boys and 63% of girls in 2001/2002 calling about running away or being homeless also talked of being abused, physically and/or sexually. Children and young people often find it hard to tell an adult about the abuse; or they are not believed.

Running from care

Jo, 13, phoned. She had just moved to a new children's home and didn't want to be there. She liked where she was before so she had run away and gone back there. When she returned to the new home, the workers really shouted at her. She left again. She said, 'I'm not going back, I can't talk to anyone there. I'd rather sleep out.'

Children running from care who called ChildLine talked of constant arguments, being hit, and favouritism for other children amongst foster carers or residential staff. They also talked of being bullied and/or abused by other children in the home, or by staff.

■ The above information is from ChildLine's web site which can be found at www.childline.org.uk

© ChildLine

Beggars hit by crackdown on anti-social behaviour

By Kamal Ahmed,
Political Editor

Aggressive beggars who intimidate people by hanging around bank cash machines demanding money are to be cleared off Britain's streets as part of a controversial new push against anti-social behaviour.

In an announcement expected in the next few days, Tony Blair will say that begging is part of a growing problem which needs to be tackled. Thirty 'intervention programmes' will be announced in cities and towns across the country aimed at clearing beggars off the streets and offering them hostel accommodation.

The Government will back local authority campaigns which say that giving money to beggars merely helps them to buy drugs.

The moves come as part of a wider campaign by the Government and local authorities to be announced on Tuesday.

Downing Street officials said low-level crimes such as drunkenness, intimidation, rowdy behaviour and nuisance neighbours were to be made the Government's 'top priority' as it tries to regain the confidence of the voters.

The plans against beggars are likely to receive a cool response from groups helping the homeless who say that Blair's tough language is demonising the poor.

'The term "anti-social behaviour" is often used as a catch-all for all sorts of seriously punitive measures often directed at the most vulnerable and marginalised people in our society,' said Adam Sampson, director of the housing charity Shelter.

The action against begging will be the centrepiece of a raft of measures to be announced in an Anti-Social Behaviour Action Plan to be personally launched by the Prime Minister.

It will be part of Blair's attempt to show that he is re-engaged with Britain's problems at home after criticism that Iraq has meant that Downing Street had lost focus on the domestic agenda.

The Government will also announce the results of the first-ever survey into the number of anti-social behaviour incidents counted by police forces and local authorities across England and Wales in one 24-hour period.

It is expected that the survey will show that on 10 September more

> *'The term "anti-social behaviour" is often used as a catch-all for all sorts of seriously punitive measures often directed at the most vulnerable and marginalised people in our society'*

than 50,000 incidents were recorded ranging from street begging to drunkenness, kerb crawling, noise, rowdy behaviour and 'vehicle related nuisance' – the use of many council estates as race tracks for cars.

Senior figures in the police service said that although the figures were useful, there were huge discrepancies in collecting the crime statistics across the country. Home Office sources admitted that the figures were 'not scientific'.

In a private summit with police and local authority representatives at Downing Street last Monday, Blair said that low-level crime could not be ignored.

Blair will urge local councils and the police to make more use of fixed penalty fines of between £40 and £200 which can be used to curb intimidating behaviour without the need to go to court.

Officers like this system because it saves them a lot of paperwork, said one police source.

■ This article first appeared in *The Observer*, 12 October 2003.

Keeping them off the streets

Berni Comissiong recalls two occasions that brought the problem of homelessness a little too close to home

The group usually took time to disperse. It was now 10.20pm and there was still a group of younger lads hanging around in the church lounge. Despite our best efforts they seemed in no hurry to leave and were now beginning to make petty excuses to stay a little longer. 'Can't I use the toilet?' . . . 'James has lost his gloves' . . . 'Is God really like that?' It was becoming apparent that there was more to their reluctance to leave than just a desire to stay in from the cold for a little longer. With a bit of probing one young lad revealed that his mother's new boyfriend was visiting, and that she had made it clear not to come home that night. He was 13 and had nowhere to go. This was the first of several such incidents that occurred in this particular youth group in a fairly prosperous town.

Several years later, I was awoken at 6.30am by an 18-year-old from my youth group. He was cold and had spent the night on the street after his mother had thrown him out. He came in and had a shower, some food and a couple of hours' sleep on my sofa. Later that day we approached his mother, who refused to take him back. We approached a local charity for short-term housing only to find that the nearest available was in the city several miles away. The young man didn't know anybody in the city and was afraid of living there. He slept on my sofa for a couple of tense and frustrating weeks while we exhausted every avenue. Eventually a member of the local church offered him a room.

The first story had a simple ending, I walked the boy home and reminded his mother of her duty of

care and warned her what would happen if the authorities got involved. This seemed to improve her mothering skills. However, as this behaviour became more frequent, we arranged a list of people in church who could respond in the case of a short-term emergency. The churches in the area began to look at housing needs, and with other agencies there were soon several projects that catered for the needs of homeless young people in the area. This included a young mum's accommodation, a short-stay hostel and some flats for single young people who required support. In addition, several young people of the church signed up as short-term foster carers, and others converted property into flats for single young people.

'I used to find it easy to throw some money to a homeless person or just walk on by'

In the second story, however, the churches worked with a local coalition, which included the education services, probationary services, police and social services to set up an emergency referral system. They then set up a campaign to lobby the local council to build relevant accommodation for young people in the town. This took several years, but it involved monitoring homelessness in the town and was an educational process for the local people and councillors.

I used to find it easy to throw some money to a homeless person or just walk on by. However, when it was somebody in my youth group, the person became real. Could I throw a 13-year-old out of church when I knew that he had nowhere to go? Could I feed and wash an 18-year-old and then send him back into the cold? Could I ignore the plight of the homeless when it was now a factor that was impacting my youthwork? Two weeks with a sulky teenager on my sofa was an extremely stressful experience. Confronting a mother and her boyfriend was a scary one. Challenging the bureaucracy or the local council was a frustrating experience. But aside from all that, I began to appreciate that 'keeping teenagers off the street' could have a far more important meaning than the traditional cliché.

■ Berni Comissiong works as a detached youth worker with Frontier Youth in London.

■ The above information first appeared in *Youthwork* magazine, October 2003.

© Frontier Youth Trust

A safe harbour

The Children and Young People's Unit has allocated £3m to fund 25 projects helping young runaways. Patrick McCurry looks at a London pilot scheme set up by youth homelessness charity Safe in the City

It's a shocking statistic, but around 77,000 children and young people run away from home every year in the UK, including 20,000 aged under 11. And many of these young runaways slip through the net of services and drift into crime, prostitution and drugs.

A report by the Social Exclusion Unit (SEU) in November 2002 flagged up the problem, and now the Government's Children and Young People's Unit (CYPU) is putting £3m into a variety of pilot schemes across England, aimed at improving service provision for this vulnerable group.

The projects, which run until March 2004, are wide-ranging and led by organisations including youth offending teams, social services departments and voluntary organisation, says Althea Efunshile, CYPU director.

'The projects are not designed for the long term, but are trying out new approaches to the problems facing young people who run away and learning lessons about what works,' she says, adding that good practice will then be incorporated into mainstream services and future policy on runaways.

One of the schemes being funded is led by Safe in the City, a youth homelessness charity, which will be working with agencies to improve the response to young runaways in east London. The £200,000 pilot will focus on Greenwich, Hackney, Tower Hamlets and Newham. It will later be expanded to all 10 east London boroughs, with a view to developing a pan-London approach in the longer term.

Rosemary Watt-Wyness, Safe in the City acting director, says: 'We want to strengthen the safety net for runaways by finding out what services are there and how agencies can work together.'

The charity's initiative is one of 25 pilots funded by the CYPU. It is based on the charity's cluster-scheme strategy for homeless and socially excluded young people. This is a multi-agency approach in which clusters are set up in a local authority area. About 30 per cent of those using cluster-scheme services are young runaways.

Clusters have slightly different leanings, depending on local priorities, but also in order to assess which models work best. For example, in Newham the cluster scheme is based on three schools, while in Brent it has strong links with crime prevention.

The clusters are one response to the SEU report, which called for a coherent, long-term approach to runaways. Its recommendations were aimed at reducing the number of young runaways, as well as making sure those who do run away are able to access services.

The report stated that there should be follow-up support for young people and their families. But it found that these aspirations have been held back by the fact that many young people and their families had not known about or had difficulties accessing services. It also suggested that those services did not work closely enough.

Safe in the City will set up working groups in each borough to identify what services exist for runaways and their families. There will be collaboration seminars for practitioners from different agencies and research into how services can be improved.

'We want to make sure there is information sharing between agencies, the right emergency response service and follow-up interviews,' says Watt-Wyness.

She adds that if, for example, the police refer a runaway to the local authority, then the practitioner

Leanne's story

Fourteen-year-old Leanne ran away from her home in Limehouse, east London, because of personal problems she felt she couldn't talk to her mum about.

'I couldn't handle the pressure that was on me so I ran away and went to my boyfriend's house, but my parents came to get me that evening,' Leanne says.

Her dad was angry and she did not want to go home, but she had to. Six months later, her problems had become worse and she left home again.

'The counselling I'd had for my problems just made me more miserable and they never really listened to me,' she adds.

After wandering around for a while, she spent the night in the stairwell of a block of flats. She later went to a police station and spent a night in the cells. The police said she should go home to her parents.

'I really didn't want to go, but there seemed no alternative,' Leanne says. 'In the end I was lucky, because my sister came and got me and said I could stay at her boyfriend's until things had calmed down.'

She feels she betrayed her family by going to the police, but says she was desperate.

'I thought if I went there, they would be able to get me a room in a bed and breakfast for homeless people, but they couldn't,' explains Leanne.

She says that agencies working with vulnerable young people need to be able to listen and understand what the young person is going through.

'They can also help by speaking to your family, because that's something I find very difficult,' she adds.

handling the referral needs to be properly trained in organising follow-up interviews with the young person and perhaps their family to avoid repeated running away.

Often, young runaways don't know how to access services, she says, but are afraid of returning home because of the reaction that they think they will get from their families.

'We want to prevent young people running away repeatedly, which means co-ordinating services and making sure young people know about them,' explains Watt-Wyness.

The Department of Health is taking on responsibility for runaways to improve coherence at national level. And locally, a named individual in every authority and police area will have responsibility for runaways.

Claire Tyler, head of the Social Exclusion Unit, welcomes the Safe in the City initiative, but says: 'Our report painted a picture of policy, social services, Connexions and the voluntary sector not working together.'

And Det. Ch. Supt Derrick Kelleher, commander of the Metropolitan Police's child protection group, also agrees that close working between agencies and local authority areas is crucial.

Kelleher acknowledges that the police's track record on dealing with vulnerable young people has left a lot to be desired, but says improvements are being made. He points out: 'Our child protection services were fragmented, which was why the child protection group was created in 2000.'

One of the main problems, he says, is that different parts of the police force have not been working together. So he has spent the past three years trying to modernise Scotland Yard's information systems on vulnerable young people, as well as trying to build bridges with agencies, through the London Child Protection Committee.

Later this year the Met will have a computerised record system for the first time. This will replace a cumbersome card-based system, and will offer 24-hour access to social services and other agencies dealing with vulnerable young people.

He welcomes Safe in the City's aim of developing closer working links among agencies and boroughs, but warns it will be difficult.

'I wish them good luck,' he says, noting that it took two years for the London Child Protection Committee to get agreement on pan-London procedures for multi-agency working on child protection. 'There's a lot of high-level policy work on runaways, but we need strong practitioner guidance.'

While most run-aways do not stay away for long and may end up living with extended family or friends, around a quarter will sleep in unsafe places

---

Among the other pilots being funded by the CYPU is a crisis-care scheme in Bradford, West Yorkshire, run by Joy Howard, the council's social services support care co-ordinator.

Under existing support care scheme, foster carers provide short breaks for families that are experiencing problem relationships. The CYPU is providing £78,000 to expand this scheme to include an emergency service for occasions when there isn't time for planned intervention.

The crisis-care service will be open to young runaways, providing a safe refuge for them as well as offering an opportunity to effect reconciliation with their families.

UK facts and figures

One in nine young people run away before the age of 16 and around a quarter of young runaways (20,000) are under the age of 11. Young runaways are:

- five times more likely than their peers to have drug problems.
- three times more likely to say they are in trouble with the police
- three times more likely to be truanting
- seven times more likely to have been physically abused.

While most runaways do not stay away for long and may end up living with extended family or friends, around a quarter will sleep in unsafe places. One in 14 runaways survive through stealing, begging, drug dealing and prostitution.

Young runaways with the biggest problems are likely to end up in city centres and spend time on the streets, sleep rough or end up with adults who may exploit them.

Adults with serious problems have often run away as children. Repeat runaways are six times more likely to abuse solvents in their life than those who have never run away.

Help, I am homeless!

Information from TheSite.org

Am I legally homeless?

Whether you are sleeping on the streets or your mate's sofa, you could be classed as legally homeless. If you qualify, you need to register as homeless with your local council.

Legally homeless

Homelessness is not restricted to being on the streets, you should also be considered as homeless if:

- You are under threat of violence from anyone who lives or used to live with you. This includes partners and spouses, be they current or exes, relatives, or anyone with legal responsibility for your children.
- You have somewhere to live, but can't stay there because of violence (threatened or actual), abuse or harassment from someone living outside your home (neighbour, ex, acquaintance) OR overcrowding or other bad conditions.
- You have nowhere to live, either in the UK or abroad.
- You live in a boat/mobile home/caravan and you aren't allowed to put it anywhere.
- You have nowhere you can live together with all your family/partner/carer etc . . .
- You are a squatter.
- You are crashing on a mate's floor or sofa.
- You are staying in temporary accommodation, such as a refuge.
- You've been locked out of your home and aren't allowed back.
- If you are likely to become homeless within 28 days. For example: a court has ruled that you must leave rented accommodation, or the people you are currently living with have asked you to move out.

Where can I get help?

Your local council's housing department has responsibilities to people who ask for help because they are homeless or about to become homeless. For more information on these responsibilities and where to find further help see the Shelter article on www.housemate.org.uk

How do I register as homeless?

If you live in England and Wales contact your local council's housing department or Housing Executive. Councils have duties to help homeless people immediately but the amount of help they offer depends on your particular circumstances. Most councils have homeless persons' sections; if yours doesn't, you should go to your nearest housing office to apply for help.

Whether you are sleeping on the streets or your mate's sofa, you could be classed as legally homeless. If you qualify, you need to register as homeless with your local council

---

If you want council housing you should make sure your name is on the council's waiting list. If for some reason the council won't add you to the list, get advice about your individual rights regarding this (Shelterline: 0808 8004444). Other points to remember:

- When you apply for council support, your case will be looked at on an individual basis.
- A housing department cannot turn you away by saying it does not help young people.
- Take along a friend, relative or advice worker for help and support.

The laws differ in Scotland. For localised advice see Shelter Scotland

What will the council need to find out?

They will want to know:

- if you are homeless
- if you are 'eligible for assistance'
- if you are in 'priority need'
- if you became homeless deliberately
- if you have a connection with its area

If you apply as homeless and the council accepts you as priority need, it must house you, even if it is just temporarily.

Am I in priority need?

You are likely to be classed as priority need if you are under 18 or have been in care; have been affected by a fire or disaster; are elderly, disabled or pregnant; are at risk from violence; have recently left prison or the armed forces or if you are under 25 and have problems with drugs or alcohol.

Important: the rules have changed. The new Homelessness Act means more people will now be classed as priority need and as such will be entitled to more help from their council. There are also new regulations for the under-18s:

Where can I sleep tonight?

You won't necessarily have to sleep rough – there are plenty of emergency options available. Call Shelterline on 0808 8004444 for immediate advice.

- Please note: This article only covers England and Wales because the laws differ in Scotland. For advice specific to homelessness in Scotland see Shelter Scotland.

- The above information is from YouthNet UK's TheSite.org web site which can be found at www.thesite.org

© *www.thesite.org*

Issues   *www.independence.co.uk*

30

Homelessness – the law

Information from the National Youth Agency

For young homeless people there are two possible ways in which the law can help you to find accommodation: the 1996 Housing Act and the 1989 Children Act. Both make the local authority (council) responsible for vulnerable people in their area, including young people.

Outline details of these laws are given in the sections below. Local authorities have a responsibility to make free advice and information about homelessness available.

There are specific points to note about the law depending on your age:

If you are 18 or over:
- If you are 18 or over you can decide yourself whether or not to leave home. At this age your parents no longer have any legal responsibility for you or legal control over you.
- If you are homeless then the local authority has a responsibility to house you under the 1996 Housing Act as long as you meet certain conditions (including living in the area, being in priority need, not being intentionally homeless and there being no other suitable accommodation which you could be reasonably expected to occupy).

If you are 16 or 17 you can leave home with your parents' agreement (consent) or if you get married (your parents have to give their consent to this too).

If you are 16 or 17 and leave home without your parents' agreement, in theory they can go to the High Court and ask for you to be made a Ward of Court, which means no important decisions can be made about you unless the Court agrees. But in practice this is rare. Your parents can also contact the police and report you as missing. In practice, if you are living somewhere, you are going to college or doing training and you seem to be safe, the police may be reluctant to get involved.

The National Youth Agency

If you are 16 or 17 and homeless it may be possible to get accommodation through the social services department of your council. The telephone number will be in the phone book. When you call ask for an interview to discuss your needs. If you need help at the interview or at any other stage of the process, go to a local advice centre, homeless project or information shop for young people.

If you are considered homeless then under the 1989 Children Act (section 20(3)), the social services department will have a legal responsibility to find you accommodation. To qualify you need to show your well-being is likely to be damaged if you don't have accommodation. There are several ways that this may be shown. It may be that there is danger in the home you left (for example somebody is violent) or that there are difficulties in your relationship with a member of your family.

If social services decide that they have an obligation to find accommodation for you, a plan must be drawn up explaining how you are going to become independent and what help you will be given for you to achieve this. A range of options should be explored, such as going back to your previous home, housing in a children's home, or council or housing association accommodation.

If you are under 16:
- If you are under 16 and you leave home, your situation may be more difficult because your parents are still legally responsible for you. Many young people in this situation end up sleeping on the streets and are very vulnerable.
- If you are staying with another adult it may be possible for him or her to apply to court for a residence order, allowing you to stay with them if there is a clear reason why you can't return home (e.g. violence). Alternatively you could contact social services and ask to be taken into care (e.g. to live with foster parents or in a children's home). The number for social services is in the phone book. It is best to seek advice if you are in this situation.

■ The above information is from the National Youth Agency's web site which can be found at www.youthinformation.com

© *National Youth Agency (NYA)*

A home should be a basic human right

A home should be a basic human right according to 90% of the British public

Despite 90% of the British public's belief that having a home should be a basic human right, almost 400,000 people live in temporary accommodation, isolated and often with little hope of finding somewhere to call a home.[1] Although 95% of all homelessness is hidden, the plight of these people is not being sufficiently addressed because they are not visible.

According to Crisis, the national homelessness charity, which today launches its campaign to fight single hidden homelessness, these people exist below the surface of a homelessness iceberg. At a time when government is close to meeting its targets on tackling rough sleeping, the charity is concerned that the desperate needs of the majority will fall off the political agenda.

The vast majority of these people are extremely vulnerable. Often they have descended into a downward spiral of homelessness as a result of bereavement, relationship breakdown, mental health problems or a combination of these factors. Lacking the support of family and friends leaves them ill-equipped to cope with these life crises.

This year, it is estimated that local authorities will have to turn away 139,260 homeless people who wish to apply for housing.[2] What is left for people without the means or the legal rights to housing and support is a limited choice between bed and breakfasts, hostels, emergency shelters, squatting and eventually, for some, sleeping rough. This is a picture of homelessness from which there can be little chance of escape. A new survey of homeless people reveals that:[3]

- The average person has been homeless for over seven years so far.
- Less than two years of that time has been spent on the streets – the rest of the time is spent moving from hostels to B&Bs, squats and friends' floors and sofas.
- 38% of people came straight from the streets to the hostel they are now in. 37% of people find themselves sleeping on the streets immediately after leaving a hostel. This is the 'revolving door' syndrome, which results in homeless people repeatedly moving from the streets to hostels.
- This is unlikely to be their last experience of sleeping rough. Over half of those people who have slept rough[4] before have been back to the streets more than five times.

This year, it is estimated that local authorities will have to turn away 139,260 homeless people who wish to apply for housing

---

It is no surprise therefore that 25% of deaths amongst homeless people occur as a result of suicide.[5] This compares to less than 1% of suicide deaths amongst the general population.[6]

Crisis believes that rough sleeping and hidden homelessness

are tightly interwoven problems and that in order to have really solved rough sleeping permanently the problems of those that exist in temporary accommodation must also be addressed.

'There is no quick and easy solution for the 400,000 homeless people whose lives are in crisis. The fact that the majority of them are hidden from view does not make them any less vulnerable than those people sleeping rough tonight. Without our help, they are at real risk of returning to the streets,' said Shaks Ghosh, Chief Executive of Crisis.

Crisis hopes that its campaign will begin to create better understanding and empathy for the plight of hidden homeless people. It is also calling on the government to look at establishing a powerful taskforce with specific responsibility of prioritising the needs of single hidden homeless people.

Crisis believes that with the right help many hidden homeless people will be able to lead full independent lives. For others, moving into permanent independent housing may never be an option. These people may always need supported and appropriate but good quality housing but Crisis believes that society has a responsibility to provide such support.

References
1 *Hidden Homelessness*, Crisis Campaign, Crisis, 2001
2 ODPM (DTLR), June 2001
3 52 hostel residents in London were interviewed for *Hidden But Not Forgotten*, Crisis, 2001
4 Nearly nine in ten people surveyed have slept rough. *Hidden But Not Forgotten*, Crisis, 2001
5 *Homeless Factfile*, Crisis, 1998.
6 Crisis, 2001.

Rooms with no view

Conference confronts rise of B&B option for homeless young

By Alison Benjamin

When Kirsti May was placed in bed-and-breakfast accommodation by Derwentside council, County Durham, the homeless 17-year-old was told that her stay would be for just a week. Then it was another week, then another.

During what became a two-and-a-half-month stay, May became depressed and dropped out of college. 'I was referred back to careers and they told me to go to the doctor as I was low and had started to take diazepam [tranquillisers] to try to feel better,' she says. 'The doctor put me on sick and prescribed anti-depressants; therefore I was left with nothing [to do] through the day.'

The worst thing about living in a B&B, says May, was that she could not eat properly. 'Sometimes, I would only have my breakfast, as I had very little money and I didn't have a cooker so I couldn't cook food. I had nowhere to store food either. I also had nowhere to wash my clothes.'

According to homelessness charity Centrepoint, growing numbers of 16- and 17-year-olds have been put in B&Bs over the past year as a result of the Homelessness Act 2002 – which extended statutory protection to this age group – and a government drive to get homeless families out of such accommodation.

By March 2004, English councils must ensure that no families with children are in B&Bs other than in an emergency – and then for no more than six weeks.

Latest quarterly homelessness data show that families with children represented 39% of all households in B&Bs at the end of March 2003, down from 45% on the previous quarter. But during the same period, the overall reduction in B&B occupancy was only 3%, to just over 12,000. 'What is clearly happening in some places is that as local authorities pursue a reduction in the number of families in B&B, young homeless people, who they are now responsible for housing, are taking their place,' says Centrepoint chief executive Anthony Lawton.

> **Growing numbers of 16- and 17-year-olds have been put in B&Bs over the past year as a result of the Homelessness Act 2002**

While May had a support worker from a voluntary organisation, the Single Homeless Action Initiative in Derwentside, Lawton's main concern is that many vulnerable young people are put in B&B without any support. 'Their needs should be assessed by social services, under the Children Act, and by housing under the Homelessness Act, but in some cases they are not receiving both,' he says.

Such concerns are being raised this week at the housing support and care conference, which started yesterday at Warwick University and is organised by the National Housing Federation (NHF). Federation members have been working with local authorities to produce strategies, required by the end of this month, to tackle and prevent homelessness.

Diane Henderson, head of care support and diversity at the NHF, says housing associations are dealing with young people coming out of B&Bs whose support needs have clearly not been identified. 'A number of members are getting referrals from young people who, instead of receiving an assessment from social services, have just been sent to the housing department,' she says. 'The government is concerned about the revolving door of home-

lessness, but without help these young people may not be able to sustain a tenancy.'

This lack of cooperation between social services and housing comes despite the Homelessness Act placing new duties on both departments to work together. John Bear, chair of the Association of Directors of Social Services' health and social inclusion committee, recognises it is a serious concern. 'If we can get the support of 16- and 17-year-olds sorted out, then they are less likely to be causing trouble,' he says. 'But carrying out responsibilities beyond care-leavers and children at risk is very difficult for social services whose resources are stretched.'

Another issue, says Henderson, is lack of integration between

> **'If we can get the support of 16- and 17-year-olds sorted out, then they are less likely to be causing trouble'**

Supporting People, the new funding stream for housing-related support, and homelessness strategies. Councils heard last month that this year's Supporting People allocation for supported housing projects was to be a third smaller than the amount bid for – casting uncertainty over future schemes.

'The Office of the Deputy Prime Minister wants Supporting People to fund vulnerable homeless groups, but new schemes are looking extremely doubtful,' says Henderson. 'We have members waiting to sign building contracts for projects that should come on stream in 2004, but, because they will not know until October/November whether funding is available under Supporting People, they are delaying schemes.'

Neil O'Connor, assistant director at the government's homelessness directorate, yesterday told the NHF conference that integrated working was essential to progress. Local strategies, Supporting People and the investment priorities of new regional housing boards were 'key elements' in eradicating homelessness.

© Guardian Newspapers Limited 2003

Stop giving to beggars . . .

Big Issue founder tells public

John Bird, the founder of *The Big Issue*, which is sold by homeless people, says the public should stop giving money to beggars as it encourages them to remain on the streets.

He also calls for laws banning beggars and rough sleepers and says legislation allowing their removal should be enforced.

But in an article for Politeia – the right-of-centre think-tank, whose patron is the Conservative peer, Viscount Cranborne – he said Britain should also be willing to provide suitable accommodation and rehabilitation for the homeless, in addition to proper care for the mentally ill.

> **'I have never met a healthy beggar who was healthy a year later. By our gifts, we give them a reason to be on the street rather than in an environment where they could be helped'**

By Sarah Womack, Social Affairs Correspondent

Mr Bird argues that current thinking on the homeless is 'very often muddled' and could even damage people who live on the street. Giving money simply maintained them in a life of disease or slow decay and death, he said.

'I have never met a healthy beggar who was healthy a year later. By our gifts, we give them a reason to be on the street rather than in an environment where they could be helped.'

Accepting that his views could be interpreted as illiberal, he says: 'As matters stand, the very notion that we should stop giving to beggars would be a cruel blow against progressive opinion that people should be allowed to do what they want.' But such a perception needed to be tackled, he said.

'It does none of us any good to watch the helpless and the needy in our doorways. It dehumanises the sufferers and it dehumanises us. The greater their numbers, the greater our indifference to them. It is not legal to beg on the streets. Nor is it legal to sleep on the streets. Various local authorities still use vagrancy and begging laws in certain parts of their city centres, but it has become less and less common to take people to court for begging and sleeping on the streets.'

Mr Bird traces the rise in street living to the decision by the Government and the police not to enforce vagrancy laws everywhere.

'We must return to the rule of law,' he said. 'Vagrancy and begging should not be encouraged. The laws do not need to be changed. They have to be enforced.'

In his pamphlet, *Retreat From the Streets*, he also writes: 'In addition, because of the trend in progressive thinking which attacked institutional care for the mentally ill, the institutions which cared for ill people were closed for those who could not look after themselves.'

He also blames the withdrawal of benefit from 16- and 17-year-olds living at home, which 'led to more young people taking to the streets'.

The upshot was that 'today we see on our streets beggars, rough-livers and distressed people, many of whom are mentally and physically ill, often with life-threatening illnesses and in a state of deteriorating health.

'They are left on the streets to decline until death removes them from life.'

To tackle the problem, he said mentally ill people should be treated as a priority and taken care of, so 'the streets are not allowed, for reasons of economy, to be places of social collapse'.

More generally, the Government should stop the need for rough sleeping by providing somewhere safe for people to go. Ministers should invest in programmes that take care of people with addictive problems.

Shelter bid to end record London homelessness

At a Shelter reception in September 2003, Mayor of London, Ken Livingstone, helped launch its revamped London services for homeless and badly housed people. The launch of Shelter's new services comes after the latest figures show that the number of people in temporary accommodation has doubled since 1997 to a record high of 55,000 homeless households.[1]

Shelter says more people will become homeless and trapped in temporary accommodation unless more affordable housing is made available. The charity also wants to see greater investment in services to prevent people becoming homeless. It says at least 25,700[2] new affordable homes are needed in London every year to make up for years of under-investment. Last year only 4,300[3] new affordable homes were built in London.

The Mayor of London, Ken Livingstone, whose draft London Plan calls for half of new homes in London to be affordable, said: 'London has twice the rate of homelessness experienced in the rest of England – and with the country's highest property prices many more people are unable to afford a permanent place to live. Shelter's new London services are excellent news for the capital's homeless and those in housing need. I will continue to work with the homelessness agencies, central government and the boroughs towards ensuring all Londoners can find a decent home.'

Shelter

Shelter which last year helped nearly 18,000[4] households in London is developing its services in order to meet the needs of the growing numbers of vulnerable homeless and badly housed people who are not getting the help they need. Many people, who are often in desperate situations, are unable to access or use current housing services or do not think anyone can help them.

Adam Sampson, Director of Shelter, said: 'It's a scandal that in one of the world's wealthiest cities over 50,000 households are homeless and trapped in temporary accommodation. Nowhere in this country is homelessness more acute and it is imperative that we deliver the homes and services that people in London need. Until then people's lives will continue to be damaged for want of a decent home.'

Shelter wants to work with all of London's boroughs and agencies to set up services that work to prevent people suffering the trauma of homelessness. It says reducing homelessness will help relieve the pressure on the capital's over-stretched housing stock.

The charity has already set up eight pilot projects targeting specific groups of vulnerable people least likely to get the help they need. These include housing and homelessness advice surgeries in collaboration with Ealing Age Concern, West Hampstead Women's Centre, City and Hackney Mind and HMP Holloway.

Shelter London case studies

Jacqui

Jacqui and her children were transferred from their overcrowded East London council flat to a house in Essex. However, the house was on an estate being terrorised by gangs of youths, who started harassing her and her family. Her front door was smashed in and her car vandalised. Fearing for her safety, she fled the area in the middle of the night and returned, homeless, to where she used to live. The council refused to help. Jacqui contacted Shelter who got a report from the Police and her neighbours in Essex, and as a result persuaded her old council to house her in a new flat.

Jon

Jon was living in temporary accommodation provided by his local council. He fell behind with his rent and faced eviction. Jon had not understood that there was a shortfall between the rent and Housing Benefit he was receiving, that he needed to make up. Shelter successfully obtained discretionary housing payment for him that cleared the arrears and stopped him losing his home. With our help he is now paying his rent in full and is now looking for a permanent place to stay.

Suzanne

Suzanne was in care as a child, and now in her early 20s suffers from depression, panic attacks, and tuberculosis. When she contacted Shelter she was living in a crowded Bed & Breakfast hotel. She was frightened and felt she was being

watched. We contacted her local council for her and got her moved immediately to a self-contained flat. We also helped her clear the rent that she owed and she has now been offered a permanent flat of her own.

Nasrin

Nasrin's parents threw her out when they discovered that she had been having a relationship with a white man. Her family and local community ostracised and threatened her. She has suffered from depression and has tried to commit suicide. She initially went to stay with friends, but they were already overcrowded. She contacted Shelter and we were able to arrange a room for her in a shared house run by a housing association.

Notes

1. ODPM Homelessness Statistics for the second quarter of 2003 (released 10 September 2003). At the end of the second quarter of 1997 there were 24,910 households in temporary accommodation

2. The Draft London Plan, GLA, June 2002
3. National Statistics 2003, ODPM. 4,329 (provisional) homes were completed by Registered Social Landlords and Local Authorities in 2002/3
4. Between April 2002 and March 2003 17,810 households in London came to Shelter for help through its London services. These included telephone advice, the Piccadilly Advice Centre, legal representation and help via its consultancy service for other advice services

■ Spokespeople are available for interview. Shelter's ISDN is 020 7251 2790

■ Shelter is a national campaigning charity that every year works with over 100,000 homeless or badly housed people through its network of over 50 advice centres and innovative projects. It also runs Shelterline, supported by Bradford & Bingley, the UK's free, 24-hour, national housing advice line on 0808 800 4444, and Shelternet, a free, online, housing advice web site at www.shelternet.org.uk. For more information visit www.shelter.org.uk

■ A copy of *Tackling Homelessness in London: Shelter's London Housing Aid Services* with more information about how Shelter operates in London is available from Matt Cornish on 020 7505 2162 or from Shelter's website on www.shelter.org.uk/media/londonservices

■ The above information is from Shelter. See page 41 for their address details.

© Shelter

Supporting victims of violence

Violent relationships are fuelling a new rise in homelessness. But while politicians recognise the scale of the problem, local support is patchy and inadequate

By Ben Jackson

Violent relationship breakdown is the reason given by nearly one in seven households for becoming homeless, and at last the issue is being recognised by ministers as a major problem.

Shelter's analysis of government figures shows that that 22 per cent (almost 28,000) of homeless households lost their home following relationship breakdown, an increase of over 7 per cent on last year. Shockingly, nearly 70 per cent of these were due to violent relationship breakdown.

New government initiatives that reflect this priority include an inter-ministerial group with representatives from five government departments, a recently published consultation paper, *Safety and Justice*, and £21 million of funding to local authorities for the development of refuges over three years.

Central to the Government's own consultation paper on domestic violence is the opportunity presented by the new Homelessness Act for local authorities to dramatically improve their approach to domestic violence and housing – a view wholly supported by Shelter.

Next month Shelter will publish its third survey looking at how successfully the new Homelessness Act is being implemented at a local authority level. It illustrates that in many cases there is still insufficient provision of services to meet local need – 18 per cent of local authorities asked had no provision of refuges or safe house accommodation at all and 11 per cent had accommodation services in place but with insufficient capacity.

However, the research also found that many local authorities are taking positive steps to develop the services they provide to victims of domestic violence.

Trafford Borough Council has recognised that domestic violence is a key cause of homelessness and developed a prevention strategy in response to this. It has formed a partnership with the local Women's Aid group in order to provide specialist support for those victims who chose not to move from the home where the violence took place. This is recognised as a ground-breaking approach. It also has expert provision on domestic violence within its housing advice service, which enables women to plan for the future in a careful and considered way – reducing the number of women applying as homeless at the local authority surrounded by their belongings in desperate crisis.

> *22 per cent (almost 28,000) of homeless households lost their home following relationship breakdown, an increase of over 7 per cent on last year*

Unfortunately, not all local authorities are so forward thinking, and this type of support and service is not available across the country. What is needed is consistency – consistently good practice across all authorities in their approach to domestic violence and homelessness. Shelter is asking local authorities to improve the way departments work together and the way they work with other agencies, to provide adequate support services, such as the example below.

One of our clients, Joanne, suffered years of abuse at the hands of her husband, leaving her and her children traumatised. When, at last, she approached her council for help when her partner threatened to kill her, Joanne was let down at every stage. Initially, she was told they couldn't help her for three weeks and to stay with relatives. She explained that it wasn't possible and was referred to Social Services who reluctantly placed her in a hotel for three nights. They then told her they would not provide further assistance.

The local authority rejected Joanne's application for housing and told her that she could go back to the home from where she had fled – they did not make enquiries regarding the violence. When she contacted Shelter we enabled her to get an injunction against the council's decision and the family is now in a bed and breakfast waiting for a final decision on their case. Shelter continues to fight for a home for Joanne and her family.

Joanne is just one voice amongst thousands of similar stories. But her terrible experience emphasises the importance and clear need for support services and housing help for those like her. With appropriate and sensitive assistance from the council and other agencies the additional trauma of homelessness can at least be more successfully handled, if not avoided altogether.

■ Ben Jackson is Director of External Affairs at Shelter. To order Shelter's fully updated new edition of *Relationship Breakdown and Housing: a practical guide* (priced £26.75 including P&P) phone 020 7505 2043.

■ The above article first appeared in *The Guardian*, 17 August 2003.
© Ben Jackson

About Crisis

Fighting for hope for homeless people

What we do

Crisis is the national charity for solitary homeless people.

We work year-round to help vulnerable and marginalised people get through the crisis of homelessness, fulfil their potential and transform their lives.

We develop innovative services which help homeless people rebuild their social and practical skills, join the world of work and reintegrate into society.

We enable homeless people to overcome acute problems such as addictions and mental health problems.

We run services directly or in partnership with organisations across the UK, building on their grass-roots knowledge, local enthusiasm and sense of community. We also regularly commission and publish research, campaign and organise events to raise awareness about the causes and nature of homelessness, to find innovative and integrated solutions and share good practice.

Crisis relies almost entirely on donations from non-government organisations and the public to fund its vital work. Last financial year we raised £5m and helped around 19,000 people.

Much of our work would not be possible without the support of over 3,700 volunteers. Crisis was founded in 1967 and has been changing the lives of homeless people for 36 years.

Delivering services

Crisis Changing Lives

A project provides financial awards to people who are homeless or vulnerably housed so that they may achieve their vocational goals, fulfil their potential and become independent. The awards help them attend a training course, buy essential tools and equipment to get back to work or start their own business. 140 people received an award in the last year across the country, an increase of 16% on the previous period. This

Fighting for hope for homeless people

programme is proudly supported by Barclays.

Crisis Skylight

This is a centre where homeless people can share aspirations, get active and be inspired. Opened in September 2002, the centre hosts a diverse range of free and practical workshops, including performing arts, repairing bicycles and yoga. Members have an opportunity to develop new or existing skills and talents, learn from one another, meet new people and integrate with the general public. By the end of June 2003, membership had reached just over 300 with, on average, 65 people attending the centre every day.

Urban village project

A project under development in partnership with the King's Fund. It aims to create an integrated community where homeless people live alongside key workers in a thriving complex of around 400 flats. Homeless people will be able to feel included in a community and access on-site services such as counselling, benefits advice as well as employment training and job opportunities. The

---

We enable homeless people to overcome acute problems such as addictions and mental health problems

---

project will also provide a high quality affordable home to people such as nurses, teachers and transport workers that are often priced out of London's housing market. Currently looking for a suitable site for the project as well as funding.

Crisis SmartMove

A nation-wide scheme which gives homeless and vulnerably-housed people comprehensive housing advice and helps them access private rented accommodation, settle down and live independently. In addition it also provides landlords with a guarantee in place of a cash deposit so that people can sign rental agreements. There are now 29 SmartMove schemes across the UK. Last year they provided housing advice to 5,959 people, an increase of over 11 per cent on the previous period. 762 of them were housed with a bond and 288 accessed other forms of long-term accommodation such as that provided by local authorities and housing associations.

Crisis Open Christmas

Open 23-30 December every year, the Crisis Open Christmas shelters provide an alternative family for many homeless and vulnerably-housed people who feel particularly lonely over the Christmas period. As well as companionship, the shelters provide people with over 20 essential services whether it's housing and benefits advice, having a full health check, recontacting their families thanks to the Internet café or developing skills and accessing further education at the learning zone. Vulnerable women, drinkers and those with high support needs may choose to go to smaller, specialist shelters. Over 1,200 people came last year and nearly 3,500 volunteers from all walks of life – 400 per shift – helped to make our shelters a success.

FareShare

A redistribution scheme of high

quality surplus fresh food from manufacturers and retailers to centres for homeless people, enabling those projects to devote more budget to other services such as advice and training. FareShare relies heavily on volunteers some of whom have been homeless themselves. Over the last year it redistributed 1,500 tonnes of food from eight depots to 214 projects around the UK contributing towards 1.2 million meals. A Crisis service since 1994, FareShare is now being established as a separate charity with continued support from Crisis with a view to provide services to other food-poor groups in addition to homeless people.

Sharing best practice
Crisis is constantly developing and adapting services to meet changing needs. Some good practice guides based on years of service delivery are available free at www.crisis.org.uk/bestpractice

Influencing and persuading
Crisis regularly commissions and publishes research, campaigns and runs events to raise awareness of the causes and nature of homelessness, to find innovative and integrated solutions and share good practice. For more information about our campaigning, research work and events, please go to www.crisis.org.uk/campaigning

Hidden Homelessness campaign
There are 380,000 hidden homeless people in Great Britain living in emergency hostels, B&Bs, squats or on friends' floors (Crisis, *How Many, How Much?*, 2003). In December 2001 Crisis launched its Hidden Homelessness campaign to highlight their plight and in the autumn of 2003 it ran a national poster and radio campaign. A series of publications have been published to map out the experiences of hidden homeless people.

New Solutions
The New Solutions research programme is dedicated to identifying the major problems facing homeless people and suggesting innovative responses, designed to enable practical, long-term solutions to homelessness. It comprises some very influential reports whose recommendations have been put into practice or been the basis of policy initiatives.

Health Action
Crisis Health Action is a specialist team within Crisis. It aims to improve homeless people's access to the full range of quality health and social care services. It undertakes research and evaluation work for voluntary and statutory agencies and produces reports, practice guides, leaflets and a newsletter to promote awareness of new solutions and share good practice.

© Crisis

Scotland moves to end homelessness

By Gerard Seenan

Every person in Scotland is to be guaranteed a home under legislation passed in Edinburgh in March 2003.

The Homelessness (Scotland) Act, passed by the Scottish parliament, is intended to ensure that by 2012 everyone unintentionally homeless is entitled to permanent accommodation.

The act, which received cross-party support and was widely welcomed by homelessness charities, is the centrepiece of the Scottish executive's social justice programme. Liz Nicholson, director of Shelter Scotland, said it was arguably the most progressive homelessness legislation in western Europe.

As well as guaranteeing a home to all Scots, it offers greater legal protection to those who are homeless or who are in danger of becoming homeless.

Margaret Curran, the minister for social justice, said the problem of homelessness in Scotland was not going to be solved overnight, but the act would tackle the root causes of the problem.

> *The problem of homelessness in Scotland was not going to be solved overnight, but the act would tackle the root causes of the problem*

'Our work on housing will go down as amongst the most significant achievements of this first parliament,' she said.

Robert Alridge, director of the Scottish Council for Single Homeless, said the act represented a culture change in the way homeless people were treated in Scotland.

'The new act aims to concentrate resources on assisting homeless people to be housed successfully, rather than on investigating how they might be rationed out of the system,' he said.

Under the new legislation, the current distinction between priority and non-priority applications for local authority assistance will be phased out. By 2012 everyone who is unintentionally homeless will be equally entitled to a home.

For people who are judged to have made themselves intentionally homeless, there will be new support in the form of probationary tenancies, which will allow them to get back into society.

There will also be changes to the process of property repossession, to help prevent one of the causes of homelessness.

© Guardian Newspapers Limited 2003

■ In an ideal world everyone would have a place to live, somewhere to be part of a group or family, a structure for human life based on a place called home. The reality can be very different. (p. 1)

■ There is no one single cause of homelessness, or any single description of a homeless person. However, there are several factors, which can lead to people being more vulnerable to losing their accommodation. (p. 2)

■ Children are the largest single group of people affected by homelessness, but their needs are often overlooked. (p. 4)

■ Each year there's less and less private rented accommodation and social housing (council houses) so it's more and more difficult to find a place to live. (p. 4)

■ Single homelessness is in the hundreds of thousands at any one time. (p. 5)

■ Despite recent, welcome changes to the legislation, there is still a real need to recognise single homelessness. (p. 6)

■ Broadly, the homelessness legislation defines a person as homeless if 'there is nowhere where they (and anyone who is normally with them) can reasonably be expected to live'. (p. 8)

■ There are only a few people in Scotland who sleep rough and are actually 'roofless'. No one is sure exactly how many people sleep rough each night. Shelter has previously estimated that, on any one night in Scotland, between 500 and 1,000 people will be sleeping on park benches, in graveyards, in derelict buildings, below bridges and so on. (p. 10)

■ Homelessness can be solved if there is the right combination of housing and other types of help for homeless people. (p. 11)

■ The causes and effects of homelessness are widely discussed. Often these are interchangeable, for example unemployment could have caused someone to lose their home, but unemployment could also be the result of becoming homeless. (p. 12)

■ Most people go missing intentionally, to escape family or other problems, but others may not make a deliberate decision to leave. (p. 13)

■ Missing people are at risk of sleeping rough. Around two-fifths of young runaways and 28% of the adults surveyed had slept rough while missing and almost one-third of young runaways had stayed with a stranger. (p. 14)

■ People sleeping rough have a rate of physical health problems that is two or three times greater than in the general population. (p. 15)

■ For an army of homeless mentally ill men and women, the parks, cemeteries and open spaces of London are the places where they live, sometimes for decades, hidden yet in plain view of 'normal society'. (p. 16)

■ The reasons people begin sleeping rough are varied: each homeless person has his own story. (p. 19)

■ You don't have to be sleeping on the streets to be classed as homeless. Street homelessness (sleeping rough) is only the visible part of being homeless and for many it is the worst. (p. 20)

■ Most people only become homeless because of circumstances outside their control. (p. 21)

■ Over 1 million 16- 24-year-olds would be prepared to suffer poor living conditions and bad landlords in exchange for cheap accommodation. (p. 22)

■ The Children's Society estimates that about 100,000 children under 16 run away from home every year. (p. 23)

■ Deciding to run is a decision made on the spur of the moment, and the young person is often not prepared, with no money, no warm clothes, no phone numbers, nor any idea about where they might seek help. (p. 25)

■ While most runaways do not stay away for long and may end up living with extended family or friends, around a quarter will sleep in unsafe places. (p. 29)

■ This year, it is estimated that local authorities will have to turn away 139,260 homeless people who wish to apply for housing. (p. 32)

■ Growing numbers of 16- and 17-year-olds have been put in B&Bs over the past year as a result of the Homelessness Act 2002. (p. 33)

■ Shelter says more people will become homeless and trapped in temporary accommodation unless more affordable housing is made available. (p. 35)

■ 22 per cent (almost 28,000) of homeless households lost their home following relationship breakdown, an increase of over 7 per cent on last year. (p. 37)

■ The problem of homelessness in Scotland was not going to be solved overnight, but the act would tackle the root causes of the problem. (p. 39)

You might like to contact the following organisations for further information. Due to the increasing cost of postage, many organisations cannot respond to enquiries unless they receive a stamped, addressed envelope.

Barnardo's
Tanners Lane
Barkingside
Ilford, Essex, IG6 1QG
Tel: 020 8550 8822
Fax: 020 8551 6870
E-mail:
media.team@barnardos.org.uk
Web site: www.barnardos.org.uk
Barnardo's works with over 47,000 children, young people and their families in more than 300 projects across the county.

ChildLine
45 Folgate Street
London, E1 6GL
Tel: 020 7650 3200
Fax: 020 7650 3201
E-mail: reception@childline.org.uk
Web site: www.childline.org.uk
Children can call ChildLine on 0800 1111 (all calls are free of charge, 24 hours a day, 365 days a year). Or write to us at ChildLine, Freepost NATN1111, London E1 6BR. Children who are deaf or find using a regular phone difficult can try our textphone service on 0800 400 222. Monday to Friday 9.30am to 9.30pm. Saturday to Sunday 9.30am to 8.00pm.

Consortium for Street Children
Unit 306, Bon Marche Centre
241-251 Ferndale Road
London, SW9 8BJ
Tel: 020 7274 0087
Fax: 020 7274 0372
E-mail: info@streetchildren.org.uk
Web site: www.streetchildren.org.uk
The Consortium for Street Children consists of 35 UK-based organisations dedicated to the welfare and rights of street-living and working children.

CRASH
10 Barley Mow Passage
London, W4 4PH
Tel: 020 8742 0717
Fax: 020 8747 3154
E-mail: crash@crash.org.uk
Web site: www.crash.org.uk

CRASH brings professionals and companies from the construction and property industries together to help homelessness charities to improve their premises.

Crisis
64 Commercial Street
London, E1 6LT
Tel: 08700 113335
Fax: 08700 113336
E-mail: enquiries@crisis.org.uk
Web site: www.crisis.org.uk
A national charity working with single, homeless people, researching, developing and funding schemes that provide help at all stages of being homeless. Ask for their publications leaflet.

Help the Aged
207-221 Pentonville Road
London, N1 9UZ
Tel: 020 7278 1114
Fax: 020 7278 1116
E-mail: info@helptheaged.org.uk
Web site: www.helptheaged.org.uk
Help the Aged aims to improve the quality of life for elderly people in the UK, particularly those who are frail, isolated or poor.

National Youth Agency (NYA)
17-23 Albion Street
Leicester, LE1 6GD
Tel: 0116 285 3700
Fax: 0116 285 3777
E-mail: nya@nya.org.uk or youthinformation@nya.org.uk
Web site: www.nya.org.uk or www.youthinformation.com
NYA aims to advance youth work to promote young people's personal and social development, and their voice, influence and place in society.

Off the Streets and into Work (OSW)
4th Floor, The Pavilion
1 Newhams Row
London, SE1 3UZ
Tel: 020 7089 2722
Fax: 020 7089 2750
E-mail: info@osw.org.uk
Web site: www.osw.org.uk

OSW provides employment training, advice, and guidance to people in London who are homeless.

Safe in the City
Unit 4, St George's Mews
45 Westminster Bridge Road
London, SE1 7JB
Tel: 020 7922 5710
Fax: 020 7928 4236
E-mail: sitc@peabody.org.uk
Web site: www.safeinthecity.org.uk
Safe in the City is leading the prevention of youth homelessness.

Salvation Army
101 Newington Causeway
Elephant and Castle
London, SE1 6BN
Tel: 020 7367 4500
Fax: 020 7367 4711
E-mail: schools@salvationarmy.org.uk
Web site: www.salvationarmy.org.uk
Carriess the Gospel to all people in every land.

Shelter
88 Old Street
London, EC1V 9HU
Tel: 020 7505 2000
Fax: 020 7505 2169
E-mail: info@shelter.org.uk
Web site: www.shelter.org.uk
Campaigns for decent homes that everyone can afford.

Shelter – Scotland
Scotia Bank House
6 South Charlotte Street
Edinburgh, EH2 4HW
Tel: 0131 473 7170
Fax: 0131 473 7199
E-mail: info@shelter.org.uk
Web site: www.shelter.org.uk
Campaigns for decent homes that everyone can afford.

St Mungo's
Atlantic House
1-3 Rockley Road
London, W12 0DJ
Tel: 020 8740 9968
Fax: 020 8600 3079
Web site: www.mungos.org
One of the largest housing charities.

ACKNOWLEDGEMENTS

The publisher is grateful for permission to reproduce the following material.

While every care has been taken to trace and acknowledge copyright, the publisher tenders its apology for any accidental infringement or where copyright has proved untraceable. The publisher would be pleased to come to a suitable arrangement in any such case with the rightful owner.

Chapter One: Homelessness in the UK

Housing and homelessness, © The Salvation Army, *Introduction to homelessness*, © CRASH 2003, *Homelessness acceptance by region*, © Crown copyright is reproduced with the permission of Her Majesty's Stationery Office, *Homeless families*, © Barnardo's, *Youth homelessness*, © Centrepoint, *How many, how much?*, © Crisis, *Housing and homelessness*, © Shelter, *Older people*, © Help the Aged 2003, *Homelessness in Scotland*, © Shelter – Scotland, *Statistics*, © Scottish Executive, Shelter – Scotland, *Causes and effects of homelessness*, © Off the Streets and into Work (OSW), *Lost from view*, © The Policy Press, *Homeless people's health*, © St Mungo's, *Rough sleepers*, © The Salvation Army, *Mean streets*, © Mark Gould, *Research challenges homelessness stereotypes*, © Safe in the City, *The needs of homeless people*, © St Mungo's, *Homelessness statistics*, © Off the Streets and into Work (OSW), *Home truths*, © Streetlevel, *Perspectives on people who beg*, © Crown copyright is reproduced with the permission of Her Majesty's Stationery Office, *Ex-servicemen make up quarter of the homeless*, © Telegraph Group Limited, London 2003, *Concerns of young people*, © Shelter, *Street children in the United Kingdom*, © Consortium for Street Children, *What happens when young people run away?*, © The Children's Society, *Family splits blamed for tide of child runaways*, © Telegraph Group Limited, London 2003, *Young runaways*, © ChildLine, *Beggars hit by crackdown on anti-social behaviour*, © Guardian Newspapers Limited 2003.

Chapter Two: Tackling Homelessness

Keeping them off the streets, © Frontier Youth Trust, *A safe harbour*, © Haymarket Business Publications Limited, *Help, I am homeless!*, © www.thesite.org, *Homelessness – the law*, © National Youth Agency (NYA), *A home should be a basic human right*, © MORI, *Rooms with no view*, © Guardian Newspapers Limited 2003, *Stop giving to beggars . . .*, © Telegraph Group Limited, London 2003, *Shelter bid to end record London homelessness*, © Shelter, *Supporting victims of violence*, © Ben Jackson, *About Crisis*, © Crisis, *Scotland moves to end homelessness*, © Guardian Newspapers Limited 2003.

Photographs and illustrations:

Pages 1, 13, 22, 31: Pumpkin House; pages 3, 8, 18, 26, 33, 36: Simon Kneebone, pages 5, 16, 25, 29, 35: Bev Aisbett.

Craig Donnellan
Cambridge
January, 2004